TALES OF
ARIZONA
TERRITORY

GOLDEN WEST
PUBLISHERS

BY CHARLES D. LAUER

Other books by Charles D. Lauer:

Arizona Trails and Tales

Arrows, Bullets and Saddle Sores

Old West Adventures in Arizona

Library of Congress Cataloging-in-Publication Data

Lauer, Charles D., 1919-

Tales of Arizona Territory.
Includes bibliographical references
Includes index.
1. Arizona—History, Local—Anecdotes. 2. Historic sites—
Arizona—Anecdotes. I. Title

F811.6.L38 1990   979.1   90-3336

Printed in the United States of America
6th Printing © 2008

ISBN13: 978-0-914846-47-5
ISBN10: 1-914846-47-7

Golden West Publishers
4113 N. Longview Ave.
Phoenix, AZ 85014, USA
(602)265-4392
(800)658-5830

Visit our website at: www.goldenwestpublishers.com

Dedication

To my wife, Mary Ruth

Acknowledgment

Most of the material in this volume came from the files of the Arizona Historical Society in Tucson, the Arizona Historical Foundation and Arizona Collection in the Hayden Library, Arizona State University in Tempe, the Sharlot Hall Museum Research Library in Prescott, the Arizona State Archives in Phoenix, and the Phoenix Public Library, Arizona Room.

Arizona Historical Society, Tucson: Biographical files of Andrew J. Doran, B. P. Darrell Duppa, Charles C. Culling, John P. Gabriel, Pearl Hart, Josephus Phy, Charles P. Stanton. Reminiscences of James M. Barney, Charles M. Clark, John F. Crampton, Andrew J. Doran, George B. Gamble, John Mahoney, Mike M. Rice. Cosmopolitan Magazine, October, 1899 issue, ephemeral files, Arizona Cities and Counties, microfilmed newspaper files. Pictures, clippings and maps from library's files.

Arizona Historical Foundation and **Arizona Collection,** Hayden Library, Arizona State University, Tempe: Reminiscences of James M. Barney and Thomas D. Sanders, microfilmed newspaper files.

Sharlot Hall Museum Research Library, Prescott: Reminiscences of Dan Genung and Thomas D. Sanders, ephemeral files, stagecoaching, stage stations, ghost towns, microfilmed newspaper files.

Arizona State Archives, Phoenix: Reminiscences of James M. Barney and Charles B. Genung, microfilmed newspaper files.

Phoenix Public Library, Arizona Room: Files of Col. James A. McClintock, Arizona historian, reminiscences of M. M. Elders, J. A. R. Irvine, William H. Fourr, James H. McClintock, Neri Osborn, A. H. Peeples, A. N. Porter, L. E. Williamson; files on Arizona cities, Phoenix, Phoenix Pioneer Days, Prescott.

Florence Chamber of Commerce: Visitor's Guide to Historic Florence.

Phoenix Planning Department: History of the City of Phoenix.

Newspaper sources credited in text. Pictures not otherwise credited are by the author.

Contents

Preface

Millions of people in America and indeed around the world are deeply fascinated by stories of the Old West, of the wild and free life on the open range, the Indians who lived there, the frontiersmen who came to it, and the settlers who established farms, ranches and towns.

It is particularly true in Arizona, one of the last territories to be tamed and settled. In Arizona, civilization is laid over the Old West like a veneer; evidences of frontier days can be found merely by leaving the pavement for a back country road, or even driving a few hundred feet off an interstate freeway. There, if one knows where to look and what to look for, the West comes to life again.

The story is not hard to find by those who persevere in their search. Many books on Arizona Territory by able writers are available in bookstores and libraries. Some were written by the pioneers of the West themselves. In libraries and historical societies are the biographies and personal histories of many of Arizona's pioneer residents, set down by them while they still lived, and collected and preserved for researchers, writers, and readers of today. Tales of ranchers and Indians, stagecoaches and freight wagon trains, outlaws and bandits, all are there in grim or glorious detail. One of the most spellbinding eras in history, that of the Arizona frontier, is there to be examined and enjoyed again.

The author is indebted to and wishes to thank the staffs of the Arizona Historical Society in Tucson, the Arizona Historical Foundation at the Hayden Library of Arizona State University in Tempe, the research library of Sharlot Hall Museum in Prescott, the archives of the library at the State Capitol in Phoenix, and of the Phoenix Public Library. Without their able and diligent aid the following would never have been possible.

CHAPTER 1

The Wickenburg Stage Road

It was getting along toward six in the afternoon of September 27, 1877, on a hot and stuffy day, but Ed Peck was breathing a lot easier. Ed was a partner in the Peck Mine, a great silver-producer at the town of Alexandra in Arizona's Bradshaw Mountains.

In Prescott that morning Ed had supervised the loading of two large, heavy bars of silver bullion from the Peck Mine into the stagecoach's boot, in which were also the Wells-Fargo treasure box and two U. S. mail sacks. The silver bars were worth three to four thousand dollars each. Peck then boarded the coach with his family, a wife and child and his elderly parents. Two other passengers, Doc Thorne and Gus Ellis, also got on. The driver set out on the Wickenburg road, curiously enough without a shotgun guard on the seat beside him. Down the road they had trundled

Wells-Fargo office on N. Cortez Street in Prescott. Gentleman seated in buggy is Job M. W. Moore, whose insurance, real estate, title and abstract business shared the office with Wells-Fargo. (Courtesy Arizona Historical Society)

unmolested, through Skull Valley and Kirkland, through Peeples Valley, Stanton and Weaver, and were now only twelve miles from their destination. So far, so good, thought Ed.

With the outline of Rich Hill fading behind it, the stage crossed a dry wash lined with cat-claw and palo verdes. As it slowed to take the bumps, two men stepped from the roadside cover with black gauze masking their lower faces, one holding at the level a sawed-off shotgun, that deadliest of weapons. No command was necessary. The driver reined in his team and raised his hands over his head. Now came the commands from the highwayman who would oversee the robbery while his partner enforced them with the menace of the shotgun.

"Get down and hold those horses still!" the driver was told, and he did, holding them by the bits though he had his hand full with the young, green, and fractious team of four. The men in the coach, Peck, Thorne, and Ellis, were ordered out into the road, the others remaining inside. Surprisingly, there were none of the usual demands for wallets.

In those few seconds, Peck had made some lightning and agonizing decisions. He could have jerked his six-gun and taken a shot at, probably killed, the road agent giving the orders. What would happen then had stopped him. The blast from the other robber's scatter-gun would have put them all at peril of bloody death. Then, too, the sudden roar would no doubt have spooked the already snuffy team, causing it to jerk away from the driver and run away headlong across the desert with the coach careening behind until it crashed with his family inside. So Ed Peck stood aside and took orders, mentally kissing good-bye his two silver bars.

There was nothing to help identify the highwaymen, their clothing just cotton shirts, jeans and boots. The one bossing the job saw to it that all the passengers' weapons were tossed away, then commanded Doc Thorne to throw out the express box and break it open with an axe which the robbers conveniently furnished. Thorne obeyed, the robbers getting almost $2,000 worth of gold dust, small gold bars, and cash. Ellis was then forced to throw down the mail sacks, and he and Thorne were ordered to slash them open and give the contents to the robber. Except that there was $600 of post office funds in one, the value of the mail sacks' contents was unknown. Then the robbers

View of the Vulture Gold Mine, discovered by Henry Wickenburg in 1863. The hoist over the shaft is at left-center, the mill right of it, and Vulture Peak in the background. (Courtesy Arizona State Archives)

considered the problem of the silver bars, intentionally cast in a weight so heavy as to discourage holdup men from taking them. To Ed Peck's immense relief, the ploy worked. The robbers decided the bars were too heavy to take, and after the usual warnings disappeared without molesting any of the passengers.

The stagecoach proceeded to Wickenburg where stage agent Pearson telegraphed the news to the Wells-Fargo agent in Prescott, F. W. Blake. He in turn notified U. S. Marshal Standefer who started out immediately with a posse, followed shortly by Wells-Fargo detective Joe Evans and clerk H. C. Meador. The sheriff of Maricopa County with two men also set out for the scene. Though Governor Hoyt posted a $500 reward for the capture of the highwaymen, Wells-Fargo offered $300 and the postal service still another reward, there is no record that the robbers were ever found.

The foregoing event was reported in the **Arizona Miner** of Prescott on September 28, 1877. According to the reminiscences of James M. Barney and other historians, Cy Gribble, superintendent of the Tabor mill at the fabulous Vulture gold mine, was not so lucky. On the morning of March 19, 1888, he emerged from the mill office carrying a black satchel that hung heavily in his hand. Gribble climbed to the seat of a buckboard, driven by Johnny Johnson, who spoke to his team, and they set off toward the Wickenburg road and their destination at Phoenix. Along with them rode Charley Doolittle on his horse, armed with a Winchester and two six-guns. Johnson had a rifle and pistol, and Gribble a sawed-off shotgun. The object of their protection rested in the satchel, a 40-pound bar of Vulture gold they were delivering to Wells-Fargo for shipment to the San Francisco mint.

Crossing the Hassayampa River some fifteen miles south of Wickenburg, they struck the Phoenix road and continued southeasterly. About half-way between the Hassayampa and the Agua Fria River was the only water between those two streams at Nigger Well. As the Gribble party approached it, and when passing a dense clump of desert growth, a fusillade of shots from ambush shattered the omnipresent silence of the desert. Johnson was killed instantly by a bullet through his heart. Doolittle, knocked off his horse by a bullet through the chest, managed to get off a few shots before, torn by more bullets, he too was dead. Gribble let loose only one blast from his shotgun before he, shot five times, was slain. One horse of the team was also killed, at the first fire.

The murderers robbed the bodies and seized the gold bar before fleeing, taking Doolittle's horse and the remaining wagon horse. They buried the heavy gold bar before taking a circuitous sixty-mile route toward the Harquahala Mountains to the west to throw pursuers off the trail, doubling back past the Vulture mine. They dug up the gold bar and tried to divide it by attempts to hack it to pieces, which failed. Two of their horses had broken down and had to be turned loose. Two of the bandits, later found to be brothers named Vegas, fled on foot and were never heard from again. The third robber, named Valenzuela, also fled with the horse and the gold bar, down the Hassayampa River in the direction of Old Mexico.

In the meantime, travelers on the road had come upon the grim murder scene and notified the authorities. The sheriff immediately took the robbers' trail with a posse, and U. S. Deputy Marshal Billy Breakenridge, once Sheriff Behan's deputy in Tombstone during the Earp years, was summoned from Tucson. Breakenridge also took the trail with three men, and they came upon the spot where the gold had been dug up while the sheriff's posse was following the trail to the west. Breakenridge and his men were now ahead of the sheriff's posse as they trailed Valenzuela down the Hassayampa. Crossing the Gila River at the spot the Hassayampa flows into it, they found Valenzuela's horse dead, caught in the quicksand, and knew that the bandit was now afoot.

Approaching the spot where a dam was being constructed across the Gila, Breakenridge trailed his man into the construction camp. As he inquired whether anyone had come into camp, a man broke and ran for the protection of some rocks. When he turned to fire at pursuers, twenty bullets struck him, instantly killing him. The bar of gold was recovered, wrapped in a blanket that Valenzuela had dropped when he fled the construction camp. It was suspected, but never proved, that the murderers were members of the Vega gang operating out of the town of Weaver near Rich Hill.

The Wickenburg road, reaching northerly to Prescott and southerly to Phoenix and Tucson, was the principal north-south route connecting those towns in territorial days, thus the most heavily-traveled. Over it poured nearly all traffic, civilian and military, whether afoot or on horseback, in stagecoaches or private conveyances, or freight wagon trains. Prescott was the territorial capital from 1863 until 1866, then the capital moved to Tucson for ten years and in 1876 back to Prescott before being settled permanently in Phoenix in 1889. When in 1879 the Southern Pacific railroad reached Maricopa south of Phoenix, it became the railhead for some time for all of central Arizona, even as far away as Prescott, and all traffic bound for the railroad was funneled down this road. And as Arizona Territory was still the Old West, full of hostile Indians, Mexican bandidos and American outlaws, travel over this or any road was chancy.

It was in the year 1863 that Henry Wickenburg, an Austrian immigrant who had been a member of the famous Peeples expedition seeking gold in central Arizona (see chapter on Stanton), discovered the fabulously rich Vulture gold mine. Having been with Peeples when the gold placers on Rich Hill and along Weaver Creek had been discovered in April of that year, Wickenburg in November was prospecting in the rugged desert ranges thirty miles to the southwest. Many are the stories of his discovery — that some prominent pioneer or other had advised him to prospect in a certain area, or that he had been attracted to a large number of vultures circling near a distinctive peak and had shot one of them, or that his burro had strayed and the gold ledge was found when Wickenburg looked for the burro. But an article in the *Arizona Miner* in June, 1868, taken from an interview with

Early-day stagecoach of the type called "mud wagon". Seats could face forward or toward both sides of the road. Note canvas top and side curtains that could be rolled down in inclement weather. (Courtesy Arizona Historical Society)

Wickenburg, said he had been prospecting with a companion, who fell ill and stayed in camp. Wickenburg continued alone, and stumbled on the rich ledge of gold ore.

His companion refused to believe that the discovery amounted to anything, and having had enough hardship, packed up and left as soon as he was over his illness. Wickenburg persisted, however, but having no money at first just sold ore at $15 a ton to anyone who would dig it out. In 1866 he sold the mine, got a $28,000 down payment, and spent it trying to collect the rest of the purchase price. He never got it. Wickenburg settled at a ranch on the bank of the Hassayampa River, which happened to be the nearest source of water for washing the gold out of the crushed ore. This was accomplished by the use of crude, home-made arrastras, and soon the bank of the river was lined with them, operated by men digging ore from the Vulture. A town called "Wickenburg Ranch" grew up, the shipping and supply point for the mine. Ultimately, "ranch" was dropped from the name, and the town became Wickenburg.

The trails between Prescott, Wickenburg, Stanton and Weaver had been developed into roads by the time Phoenix was founded in 1870 (see chapter on Phoenix). There were also primitive wagon roads from Tucson and Maricopa Wells, south of Phoenix, that passed near the Phoenix townsite bound for

Wickenburg. One of these crossed the Gila and Salt Rivers near their confluence west of Phoenix, passing the east end of the White Tank Mountains where the Phoenix Wells station was located. An advertisement in the *Arizona Miner* of June 23, 1873, read "Phoenix Wells Station, on the direct and best road between Phoenix and Wickenburg. The best accommodations for travelers, teamsters and animals. Squire and Becker, Props." Passing possibly five miles north of this road was another, along which the telegraph line was built in 1873, according to the 1879 military map.

A new and more direct road was quickly built, however, from Phoenix to Wickenburg, connecting with the roads to the gold mining towns and the Colorado River ports. Along the roads stations appeared, the principal ones as change stations to provide fresh teams for stagecoaches and serve travelers' needs. A celebrated Arizona pioneer, Charles M. "Charley" Clark, traveled from Phoenix to Prescott by stage in 1875 and named the stations he passed as Agua Fria, Wickenburg, Stanton, Peeples Valley, Skull Valley, Granite Mountain and American Ranch. The first five of these were change stations, the most important on the line.

Other stations were established, some to remain and some to disappear, as the needs of a growing volume of traffic warranted. An entrepreneur might just decide to open a station along the road, erect a building, dig a well, and invite travelers to stop. Whether it lasted depended upon the owner's abilities and the needs of passersby. Between Agua Fria and Wickenburg were Nigger Well and Lambey, near the Stanton station was Weaver, and between Peeples Valley and Skull Valley was Kirkland, among others. When in the early 1890's the mine opened at Congress, the route down Yarnell Hill was altered to pass that town on the way to Stanton and Wickenburg.

The predominant stage company out of Prescott to Wickenburg was the Arizona Stage Line, which later became the California and Arizona Stage Line. From Wickenburg it crossed the desert westward to La Paz and Ehrenberg and on to San Bernardino, California. From Phoenix to Prescott the most successful was the Gilmer and Salisbury Stage Line, with offices in Phoenix, Wickenburg and Prescott, and which furnished a connection from Phoenix to the line westerly to California. Transportation was by way of a variety of vehicles, even buckboards at first. Coaches of all kinds plied the route, including the "mud wagon" which was sort of a wagon with two benches facing opposite sides of the road and having a canvas curtain which could be rolled down in bad weather. But the familiar Concord stagecoaches soon made their appearance, and more of them when railroads were built in California. Concord coaches from the discontinued stage runs in California were sold to other stage lines still operating in other western states, including Arizona.

Availability of water, that most precious of commodities, especially in the desert, was the prime consideration for the location of stations. If there was no surface water, a well had to be dug and a good volume of water found to take care of the needs of men and animals. The first station northwest of Phoenix was the Agua Fria Station, located at approximately the spot where today's Bell Road crosses the Agua Fria River. The site was a natural, the river flowing nearly the year round. At times it and the Hassayampa disappeared into the sands in the summer, but somewhere under the sands water was plentiful, and wells sunk in the riverbed did not have to be very deep. Indeed, the *Arizona Miner* on January 20, 1872, mentioned that the Agua Fria Station was "kept by Darrel Duppa . . . who has a deep well in the bed of the Agua Fria out of which he can pump an unlimited supply of water by mule and whim power." The "whim," of course, was a circular device on which was wound the rope that raised and lowered the buckets, and turned by a horse or donkey hitched to it.

Apparently Darrel Duppa was the first station keeper at the Agua Fria crossing on the Wickenburg road, though he may have stayed there only a short time. There are enough references to his stations on the Agua Fria and New River to confuse historians and researchers, so he may have kept others after leaving the one on the Wickenburg road. As one of the founders of Phoenix, (see Phoenix chapter), he is credited with naming the fledgling town. His homestead location was bounded by the Harrison Street, Buckeye Road, Central Avenue and Seventh Avenue of today. Duppa was a wanderer, though, not the kind to settle down to the long hours and hard labor of a farmer. His actions are proof that life at the station and the opportunity to socialize with people passing by, many of them his friends, was more to his liking.

Duppa was at Agua Fria as early as 1870, according to a story in the *Arizona Miner* of September 3, 1870. A party of four men from Prescott journeyed to Phoenix to invest in the growing community. They filed claims on the site for a ditch heading on the Salt River and on ditch rights-of-way, then visited Jack Swilling at his ranch house at 40th and Washington Streets. They also visited several other old friends who had formerly lived in Prescott, including Major McKinney, who feted the visitors bountifully, and, said the *Miner,* "the number and size of the melons eaten is surprising.

"Owing to the non-arrival of a freight train the supply of stimulating fluids, in Phoenix, was extremely limited, which was regretted by no one more earnestly than by the old campaigner, Maj. McKinney, who well knows that a few drops of something stronger than water is much sought after by the dwellers in Prescott, as a preventive against cholera, fever and ague, snakebites, etc. A diligent rustling through the settlement resulted in the capture of a Mexican with part of a keg of wretched mescal, which was used as an antidote to the evil effects of too much watermelon.

"After going the rounds, the party started for home with all the melons they could take in their wagon, and arrived at the Agua Fria Station at night, which is kept by D. Duppa, formerly of Prescott. An unusual amount of travel had cleaned the station out of all provisions except onions and barley. After the party had camped for the night, D. Gibson's stage arrived from Florence —Gibson and the lady were late — all hands at the station had made their supper on watermelons. One melon was left, which unfortunately proved unripe. Duppa was suffering from a cut on his leg made by a knife in the hands of a gentleman with whom he had a little unpleasantness a day or two before, and his apologies for the scanty entertainment he provided were very energetic and emphatic.

"At noon, after leaving Duppa's, Tom McWilliams, who has a station near the sink of the Hassayampa eight miles below Wickenburg, fed the hungry party, who reached Wickenburg in good spirits and were most kindly treated by the citizens of that town . . ."

There is another reference to McWilliams' Station, reported in the *Arizona Sentinel* of Yuma on February 24, 1872: "At McWilliams' Station on the Hassayampa some ten miles below Wickenburg, on the 15th, William Bichard writes as follows: . . . I left Phoenix Tuesday at 2 p.m. Arrived at the forks of the old

White Tanks road at 1 a.m. and was chased by a band of Apaches for ten miles, but the speed of my noble steed carried me to McWilliams' Station by 3 a.m. They finally gave up the chase and waited for Mr. A. Deguerre's train of six teams, and yesterday at noon made an attack, wounding the wagon master through the arm, but the Apaches were repulsed. We have been informed that the Indians killed one mule and wounded others belonging to Deguerre." William Bichard whom the Apaches chased was a famous Arizona pioneer, owner of a flour mill and most of the rest of the town of Adamsville near Florence.

The *Arizona Sentinel,* a Yuma newspaper, carried the following on April 6, 1872: "On the 24th, Darrel Duppa at Agua Fria Station, 18 miles beyond Phoenix, was attacked by the good Tonto Apaches and slightly wounded. He and a friend were cruel enough to fight these braves and save their lives." This sarcastic report came at a time when attempts to subdue the Apaches by pacification rather than bullets was in vogue, and the Apaches showed no signs of being subjugated by any means. In the summer of 1873, apparently, Duppa moved on, as the *Miner* on August 16, 1873, carried this item: "New Station — Mr. T. S. Graves has quit keeping hotel at Wickenburg, and will hereafter devote his time and attention to keeping a first-class station at Agua Fria, on the road from Wickenburg to Phoenix. 'Old Dud' is Tim's kitchen engineer."

Next to take over the Agua Fria Station, in about 1875, was Captain Martin H. Calderwood, who had come to Arizona with the Union's California Column during the Civil War and later was stationed at Calabasas near Nogales, now a ghost town. Calderwood, responding to the needs of a growing volume of traffic, built barns and corrals, watering troughs, and improved the well system. A report of Col. H. C. Hodge, a traveler on the road, in the *Miner* of October 6, 1876, praised Calderwood's facilities. "The C & A Stage Company," said the article, "now runs a four-horse coach semi-weekly over the route from Wickenburg to Florence, 110 miles, and is doing a large business. Travel has more than quadrupled, and the four-horse coaches are now taxed to their utmost capacity most of the time.

"The coach makes but one stop between Wickenburg and Phoenix, which is at the Agua Fria, where Capt. Calderwood has a fine stock ranch, excellent water, and who sets a good table, giving satisfaction to his many guests. The captain is now about building a new and commodious house and hotel, and in a few years will, with his present good management, have a fine, prosperous establishment . . ." A highly-regarded man, Calderwood was elected to the Territorial Legislature and was Speaker of the Ninth Legislature in 1877. But on December 19, 1879, the *Miner* reported that Mr. Henry Spaulding was now the stationkeeper at Agua Fria, replacing Calderwood.

Classic Concord Stagecoach, once used by the Arizona Stage Co. Passengers often rode on top of crowded coaches. The Wells-Fargo box was stowed in the "boot" under the driver's seat. (Courtesy Arizona Historical Society)

"Our friend, Mr. Henry Spaulding of the Agua Fria Station," stated the *Arizona Miner* on April 15, 1882, "has further embellished his beautiful home by the erection of an Althouse vaneless windmill, so that the traveller can surely regale himself and beast with the cold and sparkling water for which the Agua Fria valley is celebrated. The windmill is a perfect success, running as smooth as clock work, the least puff of wind starting it . . ." In 1884 the station was purchased by M. M. Elders, who added a general store and a bar. At this time, the costs to water at the station were two bits a head for animals, ten cents to fill a canteen, and a dollar to fill a water barrel.

Some four miles west of the station on the Wickenburg road, the Hanna and Stanley freight train of three wagons was attacked by Apaches on March 26, 1871. The wagons, loaded with 24,000 pounds of wheat destined for Dr. W. W. Jones at Wickenburg, had just passed Charles T. Hayden's wagon train going the other direction, only about a mile separating them, when the Indians attacked. Five men were with the train, and defended as well as they could, but were soon in danger of being wiped out. Bill Hanna, part-owner, and three others were killed, but the remaining two, though wounded, managed to escape and overtake Hayden's train. The Indians burned one of Hanna's wagons and tried to burn the others, packed all the wheat they could on the captured wagon mules, and destroyed the rest of the wheat by pouring it out on the ground.

Caldwell, wagon boss of the Hayden outfit, at once led his men in pursuit of the Indians. Catching up with the Apaches, who were about eighty strong, the freighters opened fire, whereupon the Indians turned out the wheat they were trying to carry away, poured out a return fire, and fled with a large number of captured mules. The freighters were able to recapture only one, and were not strong numerically to engage the Indians in a general battle. The freight company, naturally, went out of business.

Though the stage companies were able to travel from Agua Fria to the Hassayampa, to McWilliams' Station or even Wickenburg without more water, it was difficult for freighters whose animals traveled more slowly and worked harder. About half-way between the Agua Fria and the Hassayampa a watering spot was finally established at a place called Nigger Well. The first attempt, and possibly the second, to dig the well turned out disastrously, but later references to a watering stop by that name indicates that a successful well was probably brought in there. Probably the well was unattended; the constant threat of large forces of Apache raiders to such an outpost in the open desert had to be a deterrent to the bravest station-keeper.

The reminiscences of the famous Arizona pioneer Charles Genung reveal how the well came by its name, and one version of the attempt to dig it. A man running a bakery in Wickenburg, who was part Negro and part Portugese, had saved some money and decided that it would be profitable to sink a well between the Hassayampa and Agua Fria rivers, to the relief of travelers across the desert between them. He engaged a helper, and went out on the road some 12 miles from the Hassayampa where he started to dig. When he was down about 25 to 30 feet, passersby noticed that the well appeared caved in and the camp robbed. No one ever attempted to clean out the well, figuring that the baker had found his grave there, and possibly his helper, too, who was never seen again.

Another version, probably an invention of some old-timer's fertile mind, was printed in an unidentified newspaper. According to the old-timer, " . . . a syndicate was formed to sink a well . . . An accident, however, which cost a . . . man his life, put a sudden stop to the work. While drawing up the dirt a heavy plank was carelessly let fall into the well and it descended on the man's head with sufficient force to mash his skull. A man went down and found that he was dead, after which a consultation was held and they decided to save funeral expenses by filling the well with dirt, thereby burying the body so deep that Gabriel's blast will hardly jar upon his tympanium.

"Another effort was made later on to sink a well some little distance from the scene of the disaster, when two other Negroes met a similar fate. Indians in those days sometimes passed through that section and while the men were working they were attacked by a band of Apaches and one of their number killed. The Indians threw the dead body in the well and it fell on the head of the man below, breaking his neck. This well, too, was filled and the enterprise was abandoned."

Genung's account is to be accepted as the credible one, the demise of the baker and his hired laborer being one of three known tragedies occurring near this spot over the years. Another was the Gribble ambush recounted earlier, and the third the murder of the Barney Martin family, also close by Nigger Well. Martin was once a station-keeper in Stanton (see Stanton chapter) who had sold out and was on his way out of the territory, when the wagon he was driving, in which were his family and all their possessions, was waylaid. All of the Martins were slain, the wagon looted, and the bodies and wagon burned by murderers suspected of being the Vega gang of Mexican outlaws operating out of the town of Weaver. Early in the 1890's speculation arose that the place was haunted.

"The four drivers who passed on the Wickenburg route between Phoenix and Prescott," began an article in an unidentified newspaper on July 28, 1892, "tell an interesting story of what may be seen almost any night near Nigger Well . . . The stage passes (it) late at night. Nearly a month ago a driver was startled by a shadowy presence which appeared at the side of the coach and seemed to touch it and travel alongside it for a considerable distance, and finally vanish by degrees. The driver at first believed this was a hallucination but it occurred so frequently that he finally spoke to another driver about it. The second driver had also seen the presence.

"A further comparison of notes showed that all had seen it. After this the shadow seemed to become more distinct and take the form of a man still white and shadowy. He nightly approached the passing coach at that point and was plainly seen to lay his hand upon the vehicle. It always vanished at the same spot. One of the drivers swore that he would take his shotgun along and on the next visitation would shoot into the fearful white shadow. The opportunity was given that night, but the driver had not the strength to raise his gun. These drivers have all related their strange vision here; they are men of undoubted veracity and courage, so considerable talk and excitement has been aroused . . . Was the white shadow seen by the four drivers that of Gribble, Barney Martin, or the unknown Portugese?"

As a relief from all this heavy drama is an often-repeated story from the reminiscences of historian James M. Barney in the Arizona capitol archives. One of the freight outfits of Goldman and Co. in Phoenix had a breakdown at Nigger Well. The driver stacked his load near the well and covered it with a tarpaulin, intending to return for it. Before he could do so, "Frenchy" DeBaud came by with another freight outfit, and noticed coyotes sniffing around the tarp-covered pile. "Frenchy" grabbed his rifle and took a pot-shot at one of them with amazing results. The cases under the tarp contained about a ton of dynamite, the shot missed the coyote but not the dynamite, and the whole load went up in a thunderous blast. Later someone asked "Frenchy" one of the most unnecessary questions in history, "Did you hit the coyote?" "Not for certaine," replied Frenchy, "but I got one damn beeg hole to bury heem in."

Beyond Nigger Well the road reached the Hassayampa River at one point of a triangle with Wickenburg and the Vulture Mine. Northward along the Hassayampa fifteen miles was Wickenburg. Crossing the Hassayampa and continuing about seventeen miles northwesterly travelers reached the Vulture Mine, and the triangle was completed by a road about fourteen miles long between Vulture and Wickenburg. The Indians, especially in the early years, were very active in attacking travelers along these roads, especially freight outfits. Not only did the freighters carry goods for plunder and were invariably outmanned by the Indian bands, the freighters' mules were a food item the Indians liked to feature on the menu. The Indians preferred horse meat to cattle, but preferred mule meat to horse meat. Even if they did not attack the freight train, they often would try to stampede the animals, including the extra mules the freighters drove with them in case one of the animals in the teams had to be replaced.

On February 6, 1869, the *Arizona Miner* reported that Rickman's freight wagon train was attacked by Indians four miles east of the Vulture mine, killing one teamster and wounding another. The Indians drove off the stock, and the other teamsters managed to rescue only five mules. Again on September 18, 1869, the *Miner* carried the story of an attack by Indians on the freight wagon train of Espirito Arriola, seven wagons and their teams, between Wickenburg and the Vulture mine. In this raid four men were killed and 63 head of mules were captured by the attackers. These instances were, of course, only two of many.

By 1878 the Vulture Mine had come into the possession of a New Yorker, James Seymour. He had a twenty-stamp mill erected on the west bank of the Hassayampa River, and on the east bank the town of Seymour was laid out for mill workers and tradesmen attracted to it. The *Arizona Miner* in the April 11, 1879, issue told of the town's being laid out at the riverside, and the May 2nd issue boasted that it already had eight saloons. The May 9th issue stated that Kimball Brothers would soon open a store there. The town never amounted to much, having only one main street and perhaps a dozen buildings, but the Wickenburg-Phoenix road veered a trifle to reach the little settlement.

Seymour as a town didn't last very long, because in the winter of 1879-80 the mill was dismantled and moved to the Vulture mine and re-assembled. The water that was needed in the milling process was provided by a pipeline across the desert from the Hassayampa to the mine, forced through the line by a pumping plant installed on the west bank of the river. The town dwindled to a stage station, corral and store run by Danny Conger and his wife, and a few residents who ran the pumping plant. Between Seymour and Wickenburg was Tom McWilliams' station to which reference has already been made and about which nothing more is known. The military map of 1879 shows Lambey's station just below Wickenburg, and there is a reference to it and Edward Lambey in the *Arizona Miner.*

Wickenburg itself was a raucous, rowdy, wide-open Western town with a full complement of colorful characters, miners, freighters, stage drivers, ranchers, and tradesmen, as well as outlaws, gamblers, saloon keepers and painted ladies. Prominent among the characters were Henry Wickenburg, A. H. Peeples who kept a popular saloon, Darrel Duppa, Jack Swilling and his partner George Munroe, Charles Genung and his family along with many, many others. As the transportation hub between Arizona's three capital cities (at various times) and the stage and freight road to California, all travelers passed through it from the humblest to the most prominent government officials and politicians, rich mine owners and capitalists, and outlaws of the most degenerate stripe. Saloons and other houses of pleasure outnumbered mercantile establishments, not uncommon in Western towns; shootings and knifings were common.

The stage road running westerly to the Colorado River and California was the frequent scene of holdups in the environs of the town itself. "As will be seen from our dispatch from Wickenburg," said the *Arizona Miner* on April 13, 1877, "the C & A stage which left here last evening was robbed, five miles out, of the express box containing only fifty-eight dollars. Marshal Standefer and John Brickwood have gone out in search of the robbers, and it is to be hoped they may capture them." Again on May 18, 1877, a scant month later, the *Miner* reported: "the stage which left this place (Prescott) on Saturday morning, carrying mails, treasure box and several passengers, arrived at Wickenburg in due time and after leaving that place and about two miles out, was stopped by four masked robbers, well-armed, who demanded the treasure box, mail bags, and the loose change on the persons of the passengers. Our sheriff, Ed F. Bowers, . . . was robbed of a fine gold watch and chain and $450 in gold coin."

Perhaps the most famous stagecoach holdup and related killings of passengers in Arizona history took place just outside Wickenburg on the California trail. Nearly every pioneer historian

This rare photo of the Wickenburg to Phoenix stagecoach approaching Nigger Well was taken by pioneer Phoenix photographer George Rothrock.
(Courtesy Arizona Historical Society)

has included his version in his memoirs. Generally it is said to have occurred early in November, 1871, but the *Arizona Miner,* which was a weekly newspaper issued on Friday, reported it in its November 4, 1871, issue and said it had occurred the previous Sunday, which would be October 30. Be that as it may, the incident was widely reported in newspapers in the east because one of those killed was a Harvard graduate considered brilliant and promising. He was Frederick W. Loring, who had been a member of the Wheeler photographic survey of geological and other prominent features of the American West. It was known thereafter as the "Wickenburg Massacre" or "Loring Massacre." Also on board were two other members of the survey party, P. M. Hamel and W. G. Salmon; Frederick Sholom, who had just disposed of his interest in a Prescott jewelry store; Charles S. Adams, founder of the town of Adamsville and at the time representative of W. S. Bichard & Co. in Prescott; William Kruger, chief of the army quartermaster department for Arizona; and Miss Mollie Sheppard, who, said the Yuma *Arizona Sentinel* on August 3, 1878, "was reputed to have amassed much money as a courtesan in Prescott."

The grim story was told by the November 4, 1871, and subsequent issues of the *Arizona Miner.* The stagecoach, driven by "Dutch John" Lanz, a veteran of California staging but making this run for the first time, was just out of Wickenburg with

Hamel and Salmon riding on top of the coach, Wells-Fargo treasure box and U. S. mail sacks also aboard. Suddenly the stagecoach came under heavy fire from roadside cover. The driver, Lanz, Salmon, and one of the stage horses were killed at the first volley. Hamel and Loring made the mistake of springing from the coach on the side from which the attackers were rushing the now-stopped coach and were quickly slain, and Hamel was scalped. Shoholm also was killed, as was Adams who was running for the protection of some rocks. Kruger and Miss Sheppard, both slightly wounded, jumped from the coach on the opposite side from which the attack came, and ran up a dry wash in a desperate attempt to escape.

For nearly half a mile the attackers pursued them, but Kruger held them off by fire from his pistol when they got too close. Then the attackers left the chase and returned to loot the stagecoach. Hours later Kruger and Miss Sheppard were picked up by the east-bound mail stage and taken to Culling's Well station. The news was relayed to Wickenburg by way of the Vulture Mine.

Two relief parties immediately left Wickenburg for the massacre scene, where they found the dead men and the looted stagecoach. The attackers had taken their booty and the remaining stage horses, and had fled in the direction of the Date Creek reservation where there were a variety of Indians — Yavapais, Mohaves and Hualapais. Kruger and Miss Sheppard both said their attackers were Indians, but there was much controversy over whether that was indeed the case. General George Crook himself made an investigation and concluded that Indians from the reservation had been the murderers. His subsequent attempts to have the savages responsible turned over to him almost resulted in his death as a result of an Indian plot, and Crook finally made a punitive expedition against them high in the mountains at the headwaters of the Santa Maria River. The pioneers, however, were almost unanimous in their suspicions that the murderers were Mexican outlaws from a gang operating out of the town of Weaver, disguised as Indians, and more than one of them was run to earth and put to death as a result of these suspicions. Miss Sheppard soon died from her wounds, and only Kruger survived.

Beyond Wickenburg toward Prescott the road veered to the northeast past the town of Weaver to Stanton. At Stanton, once called Antelope Station, there were stations kept at various times by William Partridge, Yaqui Wilson, John Timmerman, Barney Martin, Charles P. Stanton and others, a story of wild-west action and intrigue all its own, found in the chapter on Stanton. The station of Partridge and his successors may have been the change station, for, according to the *Miner* on April 13, 1877, "the California and Arizona stage company has finished the building of a new stable at Mr. Partridge's place, on Antelope Creek. Mr. Partridge is about to erect a new store and hotel, for the accommodation of the miners of the district, and the traveling public . . ." Ironically, the initials of the writer of this dispatch, signed to the article, are "C. P. S.," Charles P. Stanton.

From Antelope Station, or Stanton, the trail ascended into the mountains on a road built by pioneer Charles Genung. The next station was the Peeples Valley station, run for many years by Genung and his family. But by 1882 it had changed hands, as the *Miner* stated in its June 2nd issue: "James Hamilton of Peeples Valley keeps one of the best stations in Yavapai County." The stages stopped at Kirkland, once the ranch of the celebrated pioneer Bill Kirkland, and continued to the change station at Skull Valley. The first station keeper mentioned is Joseph Ehle in 1865. Subsequently over the years the *Miner* reported the Skull Valley station at Bowers' Ranch in 1877, then kept by John Dixon in 1879 and by Ollie Bowers in 1880. Doubtless, in later years, there were others.

The road from Peeples Valley to Prescott, and the shorter freight route by way of the Date Creek station, were no less the haunts of highwaymen than the desert trails, and fights with Indians along it were frequent. Indeed, "Skull Valley" was given its name by soldiers who found piles of bleaching bones and skulls of Indians, the results of fights between the tribes themselves. White ranchers, travelers and freighters soon found themselves the frequent targets of the warlike Indians. The *Miner* on April 8 and 22, 1871, said the wagon train of Dr. W. W. Jones and Henry Lachman was attacked by Apaches near Camp Date Creek. Lachman was killed, another wounded, and all the animals driven off in a raid on April 1st.

"The buckboard from Prescott was robbed last Sunday night, about eight o'clock, nine miles this side of Date Creek, by two Americans, one larger than the other," stated the *Arizona Sentinel* of Yuma on September 12, 1875, probably quoting the *Miner*.

"Lieut. P. G. Wood was the only passenger, and was robbed of $585 and a watch. The thieves were mean ones, even taking a ten-cent piece out of his pocket, pen-knives and tobacco from him and from the driver, and refusing to give back even a few dollars for meals. Wood had curled up on the seat and had just got asleep when he was awakened by no gentle voice, and prevented from foolish demonstrations by sight of a gun drawn down on him. He and the driver were blindfolded and made to sit down beside the road while the robbers gathered the plunder together. The latter got three bars of silver bullion and the treasure box, which had little of value in it. They did not disturb the mails. While sitting there blindfolded, Lt. Wood and the driver were made exceedingly nervous by the accidental discharge of one of the robbers' guns. Gov. Fremont has offered a $500 reward for the capture of either of the robbers."

Eventually stage robberies became so common that, unless some prominent person was involved, there was a murder or a large treasure stolen, newspapers devoted only a few lines to them, instead of prominent or lengthy stories. Thus, the Yuma *Arizona Sentinel* on November 22, 1879, said only that the stage was robbed of the express box at Devil's Gate, 15 miles from Prescott, by two men, and the letters were not disturbed. The *Miner* on April 13, 1877, said only that "the stage arriving here this morning was attacked by robbers five miles from Prescott, and the express box taken. Mail was not touched. The robbers, after possessing themselves of the box, ordered the stage to drive on. No clue to the robbers, as they were masked closely." Wells-Fargo eventually discontinued its express service from Prescott to the railhead at Maricopa because of losses to robbery.

The last station before reaching Prescott, the American Ranch, was twelve miles out of town and kept at least for a time by J. H. Lee. The *Miner* on June 6, 1876, stated that Lee was building a new house and station, and devoted considerable space to describing it. "When completed," added the *Miner*, "Mr. Lee proposes to open it as a hotel for the accommodation of travelers, teamsters, and others . . . About the 25th of July he expects to have it so far completed as to give a grand ball and excursion, at which time he will have boats on the lake for sailing, etc.," all of which sounds pretty plush for the frontier in 1876.

When the Congress Mine opened in the early 1890's and the stage road passed by the town that sprang up there, at the foot of

Yarnell Hill, another station came into being, though there had been a small one at nearby Congress Junction for some years. It was called Martinez Station or Martinez Ranch, after the first known man to settle there. In the spring of 1871 the California and Arizona Stage Company kept two men and four horses there as a change team. Four Mexicans camped nearby one day attacked the little station, killed the keeper, Sam Cullumber, and slit the throat of the stock tender. The Mexicans took the four horses, along with some loot, and headed for the border. At Phoenix they paused to rest, and were spotted at a canal bank by a Maricopa Indian who reported what he had seen to the authorities. Deputies Joe Phy and Milt Ward investigated, followed the murderers, and came upon two of them sitting on a log beside the road.

Phy ordered the fugitives to throw up their hands, but instead they reached for their six-shooters. Ward gunned down one of them with a shotgun, but Phy broke the other's gun arm with a rifle bullet. The Mexican picked up the gun with his left hand, whereupon Phy broke his left arm with a bullet. Then the man tried to run for the riverbank only a few steps away, and Phy broke his leg. According to reminiscenses of Dan Genung, "he would not tell anything about it and only begged for water . . and is begging for water yet, I guess."

An article clipped and filed from an unidentified newspaper states that on September 21, 1894, the stage left Congress driven by veteran Andy McGinnis, and with only one passenger, J. F. Michaels of Williams. The road for some distance was a sharp, steep, stony grade, and after only a few hundred feet the stage's wheel struck a rock, throwing the driver to the ground. The spooked team ran away, down the rocky road. The passenger did not understand the situation at first, trying to hold on to the crazily rocking coach. He recovered his wits, and leaning out the window shouted "Whoa!" as loudly as he could. That did it. One of the lead horses swerved and fell, the coach ran over it, the other horses were tangled in the wreckage. Michaels came out of it safely, but the driver had suffered a fractured skull, of which he died. Accidents were not uncommon, road conditions being what they were, just routine. For example, witness the item in the *Arizona Sentinel* on January 3, 1880, that "the southbound stage was late, having upset yesterday in the bed of the Hassayampa River."

The stage southbound from Prescott was making a night run on September 10, 1894, with six passengers on board. Four of them were prominent men in the territory and important in the Republican party, bound for the party's convention at Tucson. They were J. C. Martin, editor of the Prescott *Journal-Miner*, C. M. Funston, editor of the Flagstaff *Sun*, A. J. Doran, former sheriff of Pinal County, and Dr. George W. Vickers. Carl Hazeltine and one Park were the other passengers; Martin was riding on the outside seat with the driver. According to the *Journal-Miner* of September 11, the stagecoach reached a big gulch two miles below Congress, when "a lone highwayman gracefully stepped from behind his cover and commanded a halt. It was instantly obeyed." Martin, however, had the presence of mind to drop his wallet under the seat as he was climbing down, and Vickers and Hazeltine to drop their gold watches in the seat of the coach.

"(The highwayman) then asked the occupants to step out, which was obeyed likewise with alacrity, one by one . . . "Gentlemen, I will examine your credentials, and in the meantime you may elevate," was his salutation. Of course this was also obeyed (hands up) . . . Doran was the first victim. He made short work, and after taking his gold watch, pocket book and other wares, asked him if he had any proxies. He answered 'no.' Vickers was number two, and the way he went after the doctor was really ludicrous. He knew the doctor was loaded, and the latter was permitted to lower his hands to take off his boots, in order that nothing could be concealed. The doctor obeyed with a grunt, and on mentioning Oakes Murphy's name was told to shut up. (Murphy was Governor of Arizona Territory at the time.)

"I'm on to you," was the greeting of the highwayman to J. C. Martin. "You roasted me once and now I'll play even. Get out your subscription book and don't overlook any proxies, either." With Martin he was particularly severe, going through him twice and telling him he was a chump to travel on a stage when he had a pocket full of railroad passes. From Martin he got ten silver dollars, which seemed to please him immensely. "I had a watch," Martin said later, "in fact, I never thought of the watch until the fellow had it out of my pocket. I stood at the head of the class, and after he had made the rounds of all of them, he started in again and asked if I did not have something else . . . Just then he commenced to unbutton my coat, and I thought he intended to search all my pockets, but he was just unhooking the watch chain, yanked it out of my pocket and slipped it down into his."

"When Editor Funston was reached," continued the *Journal-Miner*, "there was a weakness noticeable in his victim, and telling the skylight journalist to look through the Lowell telescope for a few seconds, he pillaged this poor editor of all he had — a dollar in cash, a watch, and seven Republican proxies. Uttering an oath, the highwayman sized up the other two and asked them if they were politicians, to which they answered 'no.' He was merciful, and only made a partial cleanup on these miners. He asked the driver his politics, and on being informed that he was a Democrat-Populist, he was complimented by the political holdup.

"After securing five gold watches, $600 in cash and 37 proxies, (the robber looked into) the coach, and spied a sack on the seat, which he demanded, but it was so heavy that it took two men to lift it. The bandit almost fainted when he beheld it, as also did the delegates when it vanished." In it was $5,000 in campaign contributions, doubtlessly in weighty gold and silver used almost exclusively then, and more convention proxies. "The driver was told to move, and with echoes filling the air of populism and democracy, the first political holdup of the season ended, and successfully, too, for the enemy. Today, the wires are being burned up with messages of condolence and offers of assistance, and a new subscription is being talked of to keep up the dignity of the brethren in a strange land, where even hand-outs are unknown, and where no ray of sunshine is ever extended to a body of busted delegates." Especially, it might be noted, to Republican delegates in heavily-Democratic Tucson.

Later stories said the trail of the robber(s) led directly to Congress after the holdup. A few days later Hazeltine, a bookkeeper at the Congress mine, received a letter containing $5.00 and a note in the mail, signed "robber no. 2," saying they did not want his money. This confirmed a theory that there were two robbers, living at the Congress mining camp. It was thought that they were in the camp when the stage went through, went to the robbery scene while the mails and baggage were being transferred, and immediately after the robbery back into the camp.

Considerable merriment grew out of this robbery, since no one had been injured. One wag said Oakes Murphy felt safer with those proxies in other hands, and hired the highwayman to capture them and vote them in person. Another said it was a put-up job between Martin and Funston to get away with the campaign sack. Still another claimed that Martin insisted on keeping four dollars and sending the robber the weekly *Journal-Miner* for one year, which offer was declined with thanks. Martin and Funston, at any rate, returned to their homes by taking the train from Tucson to Los Angeles, where they transfered to trains coming over northern Arizona, to Ash Fork and Flagstaff.

The invention of trains and establishment of railroad lines were the beginning of the end for stagecoach lines, of course; they were polished off by the invention of the automobile. For an interim period the stagecoach lines operated where the railroad had not yet reached, until spur lines were built eventually even to the remotest regions. The Southern Pacific line built across southern Arizona in 1879 had a station at Maricopa, sixteen miles south of Phoenix, which became a terminal for central Arizona stagecoach passengers and freight. The Atlantic and Pacific line across northern Arizona reached Flagstaff on August 1, 1882, its station at Ash Fork providing a terminal for the Prescott area.

The legendary, long-time superintendent of the Gilmer and Salisbury Stage line, who also became superintendent of the California and Arizona Stage line, was the unchallenged czar of stagecoaching, from Prescott to Wickenburg to Phoenix and Florence, for twenty-five years. The *Arizona Miner* of Prescott on April 13, 1877, carried this article: "James Stewart, superintendent of the California and Arizona Stage Company, . . . is increasing the stock on the railroad (connection in California), has put the trips from Wickenburg to Florence tri-weekly on and after the 15th, and has changed the time of leaving here from six in the evening to seven in the morning . . ." He was keeping an eye on the railroad two years before it reached here. As it was building across the state in 1879, the following appeared in the *Miner* on March 21, 1879:

"James Stewart, superintendent of Gilmer and Salisbury's stage line, has decided to connect with the Southern Pacific railroad at Gila Bend. Mr. S. has been over the ground and decided that Gila Bend is several miles nearer Prescott than Maricopa Wells, hence the change to Gila Bend. It is estimated by careful, reliable persons that the distance from Prescott to the Southern Pacific at the point selected by Mr. S. can be reached in

125 miles. If this is correct, then it would be 20 miles nearer than Maricopa Wells." In actuality, the railroad never reached Maricopa Wells, passing eight miles south of it to Maricopa Station, adding those eight miles to Stewart's calculations. He never carried out his plan to connect at Gila Bend, either, coming to the sensible conclusion that the road south through Phoenix and the other stations along the road to pick up passengers was a better idea. There were already facilities at those stations and Phoenix, too, while the trip to Gila Bend would have meant building a new road and establishing new stations across 125 miles of waterless desert.

The road between Phoenix and the Maricopa railroad junction was always a popular place among road agents also, and the stagecoaches were regularly robbed, despite the best efforts of the constabulary. Witness this item in the Yuma *Sentinel* on May 10, 1879: "The stage was stopped three miles south of Phoenix on Monday, at 2:30 a.m., by a single man. He took only the express box without disturbing mail or passengers." On June 28, 1879, appeared this article: "Phoenix, June 21. The south-bound stage was robbed last night at 10 o'clock, three miles south of here, by one man who took the mail and express box. The mail bags were recovered but the box could not be found. A reporter visited the spot and is of the opinion that the robber is the same one who robbed the stage two months ago. "Mac" ought to remember the spot, for "he was there." We understand that Mr. Stewart, agent of the line, was driving this time, and that there were three passengers." It is not at all odd that James Stewart, superintendent of the line, was the driver, as agents frequently had to substitute for drivers who did not appear, or showed up in no condition to take a stagecoach out on the road.

You can still travel the old Wickenburg road, approximately, all the way from Prescott to Maricopa. From Prescott you take the Iron Springs Road out of town, past Woolsey's hill to the hamlet of Skull Valley, then on to Kirkland where there is a cowboy bar but not much more. From there you go to Kirkland Junction on the Highway 89 of today and south through Peeples Valley to Yarnell. The road here is approximate, as the highway builders have straightened it out. From Yarnell in a pickup truck or four-wheel drive vehicle you could take the old back road, built by Charles Genung, down the mountain to Stanton. Most people, though, would stay on the highway down Yarnell Hill to Congress which once was Congress Junction. The ghost town at the Congress Mine is three miles to the north of this point.

Just before entering Congress Junction a road sign points toward the ghost towns of Stanton and Weaver, and there is a dirt road across the desert from Weaver to Wickenburg. If the traveler does not want to chance this, Highway 89 heads to Wickenburg, southwest of which the old settlement at the Vulture mine is maintained as a museum. Out of Wickenburg, Highway 89 closely follows the old road down the Hassayampa River for a time, then veers off across the desert. Nothing marks the location of Nigger Well. At the point the highway crosses the Agua Fria River near Sun City, Darrel Duppa and his successors ran the old station. You are still on the old road down Grand Avenue into central Phoenix, at Seventh Avenue and Van Buren, where you take Van Buren to Central Avenue and drive down Central to Adams Street. On the southeast corner of Central and Adams was the stage corral and office, taking in the entire quarter of the block. The office stood at the corner of the alley between Adams and Washington on Central.

The old desert road past the Phoenix townsite has long been obliterated, but you can go south on Central to Baseline Road, then east to 56th Street and the Yaqui village of Guadalupe. Turn south and you are on the road to Maricopa, crossing the freeway at the border of the Pima Indian Reservation, and continuing south on the Maricopa Road across the reservation to the town of Maricopa itself, a hundred years ago the connecting point for Phoenix with the Southern Pacific railroad.

If you ever take this drive, "appreciate" while you do. Along this road from Prescott to Wickenburg to Phoenix at one time traveled every forefather of this state. Everyone, of high station or low, on foot or horseback, in freight wagon, or stagecoach or private vehicle, traveled along it as you are doing, saw the same desert and mountain landmarks, and for this time you are one with them. Probably some of the same great saguaro cacti they saw, because of the saguaro's longevity, we also see. The presence of Governors John C. Fremont and Anson Safford, of Buckey O'Neill and Will Barnes, Wyatt Earp and Doc Holliday, Ed Peck and Cy Gribble, even of Carl Hayden and Barry Goldwater, still is felt along the Wickenburg road.

CHAPTER 2
Stanton and Weaver

If you hang around ghost towns long enough to become familiar with the history of a number of them, you may be struck by their resemblance to the lives of outlaws who once haunted many of them. They may have been conceived in unknown circumstances (maybe even accidentally), they shot up in childhood and matured so fast as soon to become too big for their britches, their youthful years were occupied by wild and uncontrolled lawlessness and the most barbaric dissipations, their declining years were marked by submissiveness to others who had become more powerful, and at the end they disappeared completely, unknown and unmarked, or lingered as living shells of their dead glories.

That is an apt description of two central Arizona ghost towns, close by each other, which you will soon discover if you persevere. They were spawned by the discovery of the third deposit of rich placer gold in Arizona. The first was at Gila City a short distance east of the present Yuma in 1858, where Jacob Snively found

Ruins of a stone house, the only remains of the town of Weaver, Arizona, to be found in 1988.

gold placers along the Gila River. The second was in January, 1862, when a party of trappers led by the famous scout Pauline Weaver discovered placer gold along the Colorado River, and the town of La Paz sprang up nearby. The third was that found in the tale upon which we are about to embark, and the towns of Weaver and Stanton.

It all began with a "forty-niner" named Abraham H. Peeples, a North Carolinian who early in 1863 found himself washing very poor gravel in the Kern River in Tulare County, California, and resolved to do something about it. Hearing stories of the gold strikes in Arizona, he persuaded two associates, Joe Green and Matt Webber, to accompany him to Arizona to try their luck. Arriving at Fort Yuma, they received a quick education about the kind of terrain they would find and the hostile Indians that inhabited it. They then sought to enlist some companions in the venture, and as luck would have it their first and most important recruit was none other than the redoubtable scout, Pauline Weaver, he of the La Paz placer discoveries.

In the files of the eminent Arizona historian James H. McClintock is found the first-hand account of the organization of the Peeples expedition and its gold discoveries, from an interview with Peeples himself. Weaver was already a man well advanced in years. He had spent a long time in southern Arizona, mostly as a trapper. He was highly esteemed by the Indians along the Colorado River, and by the Pimas and Maricopas of the interior, and was able to converse fluently in several Indian tongues. "We were delighted to gain Weaver for one of our party," said Peeples. "Though he had never dared to visit central Arizona where we proposed going, we knew we had struck just the right man for our purpose.

"We were fortunate in finding him at Fort Yuma. He very rarely came to the settlements, but just then he was completing a treaty of peace between the Pimas and Maricopas and the Mohaves, being implicitly trusted as an arbitrator of the differences between the two parties. He was anxious to go, but we had difficulty in making up any considerable force. Finally we convinced to accompany us an educated German named Henry Wickenburg, a stout Negro named Ben, a young Mexican, and three Americans whose names I cannot call to mind. I had a complete diary of the trip, but it burned up about ten years ago (what a tragedy!). I know one thing, however, . . . it was a fine lot of men, ready and fully equipped to meet any danger."

The party started north along the Colorado River about April 1, 1863, until they struck the Bill Williams Fork. There was water in the fork at that time, and eastward along it they traveled about fifty miles, prospecting as they went. They had left the stream but a few days when they camped on the slope of a mountain about eighty-five miles north of the present location of the city of Phoenix. "I here killed three antelope," continued Peeples, "and we gave the peak the name it now bears of Antelope Mountain (Antelope Peak). I jerked the meat, and while it was drying a few of us went prospecting in the near neighborhood. As luck would have it, we struck it rich in the creek bed the very first day.

"It does seem odd that we had made a course as straight as could be run to the very richest placers that have ever been discovered in Arizona. Curiously enough, though, the best ground was right on top of the mountain. Of course there was no water there, so we sorted over the ground for the coarser pieces of gold and packed the finer dirt down to the creek to wash in California style. To show how rich the ground was, I remember one day that only three of us were at work, the others going off about something else. By just scratching around in the gravel with our butcher knives, we obtained over $1,800 worth of nuggets before evening. We didn't do that well every day, but the amount that was taken out was something immense." Which led, of course, to the other name by which the mountain is known — Rich Hill.

It wasn't long before supplies began to run short, and it was determined to go to Maricopa Wells for more. Moreover, the Apache Indians were becoming increasingly active in the vicinity, and the Peeples party of ten felt itself inadequate to defend the diggin's with that few. Maricopa Wells was then the most important location in central Arizona, a large and well-stocked stagecoach station on the overland trail. Weaver, who had been elected captain, knew the general direction of the Wells, but the country between was a blank to everyone. Following the Hassayampa River downstream, they left it below a box canyon, and struck out across a sixty-mile desert at night. They passed east of the White Tank Mountains and came to the Salt River near its junction with the Gila River. There they saw some Pima Indians.

Soon they were at Maricopa Wells, now an abandoned ruin on

The original Stanton Hotel in the town of Stanton, Arizona, as it appeared in 1988.

the Pima Reservation south of Phoenix and about eight miles north of the hamlet of Maricopa. A number of men were at the Maricopa Wells station, among them the well-known Jack Swilling. One look at the pokes of gold dust, along with the stories of how plentiful it was, made Jack only too anxious to join the party on its return trip to the diggin's, which he and others did. Along the stage line east and west of Maricopa Wells the magic message flowed, "Gold discovered!" Soon men were flocking to the "Weaver District," in sufficient numbers to defy the Apaches, and were busily washing the gold out of the creek bed and scraping it from the crevices of Rich Hill.

The men of the Peeples party had renamed the creek "Weaver Creek" in honor of their guide, and soon on its banks was growing a community called Weaverville at the beginning, but later shortened to just Weaver. Over Antelope Mountain (or Rich Hill) to the northwest about four miles other placer deposits were found along Antelope Creek which soon attracted more gold washers. Near these placers another community grew, at first known as Antelope Station because the stage route from Wickenburg to Prescott, by way of Weaver of course, wound through it on its way up the tortuous incline of the Mogollon Rim to Yarnell on its way to Prescott.

Soon after the ascent, the stage road crossed a long, lonely valley, perfect for raising cattle, and here A. H. Peeples settled and took up residence. It was, and is, known as Peeples Valley. Peeples did not stay forever, though. Eventually he moved on, was for a long time a keeper of a popular saloon in Wickenburg under his name, lived for a time in Phoenix, and even bought the Tyson Wells stage station near today's town of Quartzsite on the La Paz to Prescott road. Peeples sold his ranch to pioneer Charles B. Genung, a fine and courageous man, who eventually figured prominently in the fates of Weaver and Antelope Station.

The stage was set for the entrance of the villain of the drama to follow. His name was Charles P. Stanton, as unprincipled a ruffian as ever walked the earth. The illegitimate son of an Irish lord, Stanton had studied for the priesthood, but was dismissed from the order, some sources say for "immorality" and others for absconding with the monastery's funds, but probably both. To escape the authorities, he fled to America. In Denver he was caught in another scam involving fake gems, and thought it wise to escape to the anonymity of the Arizona desert. He arrived in Arizona in 1871, and found employment at the Vulture Mine near Wickenburg as an assayer. There he made the acquaintance of a prospector named Dennis May. Dennis was the discoverer of the rich Congress gold mine, north of Wickenburg and only some eight miles from Weaver and Antelope Station. Dennis May also had a gold claim named the "Leviathan" only a couple of miles from Antelope Station. Stanton, it is said, told May no one would be the wiser if he just passed up doing his yearly assessment work on the Leviathan. Then he blackmailed May into giving him a half-interest in the claim not to tell anyone about it.

May eventually sold his half-interest in the claim, but Stanton retained his, and took up residence nearby. He built a dwelling, in which he also operated a store, at Antelope Station, which gave promise of becoming a prosperous village. Aside from the placers which were still being worked, the town of Weaver a couple of miles away at the original placers discovered by the Peeples expedition was gaining a bad reputation. There the diggin's were becoming worked out, and the town had been taken over by a gang of outlaws. Its leader was Francisco Vega, a ruthless butcher devoid of any shred of compassion or principle. He and his men

Saloon and dance hall building still stands in the town of Stanton, Arizona, 1988. Sign was attached by the current owners of Stanton townsite.

were responsible for years for thievery, robbery, stage holdups and rustling all over Arizona and New Mexico, even beyond. Responsible citizens and businesses were avoiding Weaver, but were becoming attracted to Antelope Station.

The stage station there was operated by G. P. Wilson, better known as "Yaqui." Yaqui Wilson had acquired that name and become something of a local celebrity by helping the Yaqui Indians of Old Mexico in their struggle. The government there had tried to exterminate them, deporting a large number from their traditional homeland in Mexico's south to its northern desert. Yaqui had led them in some of their battles in Sonora, but at length sought refuge in America and settled at Antelope Station. His stage station and store were popular and well patronized, though there was another stage station and store in the little settlement run by William Partridge. Theirs was a lively competition, but Stanton coveted their businesses for his own.

Always maintaining the facade of the solid businessman and community leader, Stanton was secretly following his own devious paths. He had made friends with the outlaw chief, Vega, and arranged to have Vega's gang do some little jobs. And he slyly promoted a feud between Wilson and Partridge. When one day Wilson's hogs got loose and ate up some of Partridge's supplies, Stanton secretly had a member of the Vega gang advise Partridge that Wilson was out to get him. Then Stanton advised Wilson to settle up with Partridge and pay for the damage his hogs had done. Unarmed, Wilson approached Partridge's place on his mission of good will, but Partridge was waiting with a gun and, without warning, shot Yaqui Wilson dead.

Partridge hid out for a while, but finally sought the advice of Stanton, which was to give himself up. Pausing at the Genung ranch home in Peeples Valley long enough to turn in his gun and tell his story, Partridge took the stage to Prescott and surrendered to the authorities. He was tried, convicted, and sentenced to life imprisonment in Yuma Penitentiary. The way seemed to be clear for Stanton to take over the stage station business. Imagine his consternation when a man named John Timmerman arrived, asserted that he was Yaqui Wilson's silent partner having loaned him some of the money to go into business, and re-opened Wilson's place himself. Then some of Partridge's creditors got together and installed one Barney Martin in Partridge's old store and station, to operate it so they would not lose their money.

Charles Stanton was forced to lay low for a time, to protect his image as a respectable businessman. In March, 1875, a post office was granted the community and it was re-named Stanton, replacing Antelope Station. The postmaster appointed was, of course, Charles P. Stanton. For ten long years he had to content himself with being the brains behind Francisco Vega's gang of

Rich Hill (Antelope Mountain) as seen from the site of the town of Weaver. In left foreground is Weaver Creek.

cutthroats operating out of Weaver, while both Timmerman and Martin prospered, and Martin's family grew up in the face of mysterious adversity. Twice Barney Martin's station burned down and was rebuilt. On both occasions Stanton was suspected of arson on circumstantial evidence, and on one of them the superintendent of the stage line, James Stewart, removed an employee to a safer town after he had seen Stanton running from the scene of the fire. Stewart knew that the life of a witness was no longer secure.

One day John Timmerman, who was running Yaqui Wilson's old station, left for Wickenburg with $700 in gold. He was on his way to send it by Wells-Fargo express to a liquor dealer in San Francisco to whom he owed the money. On his way he was ambushed, killed by a shot in the back through his heart, and robbed by someone who then poured oil on his clothing and set him afire. A traveler on the road happened by while the fire was still burning and put it out, but of course Timmerman was dead. Charles P. Stanton produced a will naming him the beneficiary of Timmerman's estate, acted as executor, and took over his business.

Years later a member of the Vega gang named Juan Reval was in prison on another charge, and before he died he confessed to being Timmerman's killer. He revealed that Stanton had watched the crime from a hiding place near the road and had received half the money Timmerman was carrying. Reval at the same time implicated Stanton in the robbery of a Prescott-Ehrenberg stage between Date Creek and Culling's stage station on the desert. Stanton planned the holdup, in which three bars of silver bullion were taken. Jim Hume, chief detective of Wells-Fargo operating out of San Francisco, was called in to investigate. He recovered one of the silver bars from the leader of Vega's gang that pulled off the job, and in searching for another, Hume had the floor of Stanton's house torn up. Under it was a cache of rifles stolen from Bradshaw City. Another bar was melted down by the gang, their share of the loot.

It was the mass murder of Barney Martin and his family, however, that was the most loathsome deed of Stanton's criminal career. Warned time and again that he and his family were in danger, and having enough of his buildings being burned and his possessions stolen, Barney Martin finally sold out, loaded his baggage and his family into a wagon, and in July, 1886, set out for

Maricopa rail depot south of Phoenix. There they intended to take the train to Ohio. Before leaving, Martin had notified a friend, Captain Martin Calderwood, who ran the Agua Fria stage station on the Phoenix-Prescott stage road, that he would stop with him for a visit.

The Martin Family was also to have met Charles Genung, he of the Peeples Valley ranch, en route to allow Mrs. Martin and her children to travel in Genung's more comfortable buggy. Genung was held up in Prescott by court business, and the connection was never made. Just south of Wickenburg the Vega gang ambushed the Martin wagon and forced Barney Martin to drive to a mesquite thicket near the present location of Morristown. Vega himself was with the gang, and one Elano Hernandez was doing the actual dirty work, while Stanton followed and watched the murder from a hilltop.

Hernandez ordered Martin to halt the wagon and get down. As he did so, Barney reached for his gun, whereupon Hernandez stabbed him through the heart. Mrs. Martin climbed down from the other side with her children and begged Vega to spare her life, but as she dropped to her knees, Vega pulled her head back by the

Dan Genung in Weaver, using rocker to look for gold at the base of Rich Hill (right, background). Photo taken in 1913. (Courtesy Arizona Historical Society)

hair and Hernandez cut her throat. He then slit the throats of the two boys, the bodies were scalped to make it appear to be the work of Indians, they were thrown into the wagon, covered with brush and set afire. On its return trip, the gang stopped at the house of a Mexican woman where they obtained food and liquor. The woman was able to gather from their conversation, particularly after the liquor had taken effect, what they had done. Unknown to the outlaws, the Mexican woman was a friend of Genung, whom the gang had expected to catch and murder during their ambush of the Martins.

When the Martins failed to appear at his station, Calderwood notified Genung, who then asked around among other friends of the Martin family. He then notified Maricopa County Sheriff Noah Broadway, who assigned Deputy Billy Blankenship to investigate. Blankenship and Genung took the back trail and scoured the desert, but it was Fritz Brill who had a ranch south of Wickenburg that came upon the scene of the murder. Finding wagon tracks in an unusual place, he followed them and found the remains of the burned wagon and charred bones of the Martins. He salvaged what remains he could and buried them on his ranch.

Following the trail of the outlaws' horses from the scene of the crime, Genung and Blankenship came to the house of the Mexican woman where the gang had stopped. From her they learned the identity of the criminals, and the story of the murders she had pieced together. Elano Hernandez was arrested and taken to Phoenix, where he was bound over to the grand jury, but for some reason was released. Furious, Genung then had Stanton himself arrested and taken to Phoenix, but Stanton was eventually released for lack of evidence. By this time, however, his reputation as a respectable businessman was pretty well blown amid rumors of his criminal involvements. Those close to the situation knew him for what he was, and the day of reckoning was at hand for Charles P. Stanton.

In Stanton lived the Lucero family, with three brothers, Pete, Chano and Sesto, and a beautiful daughter named Froilana. Some months before the Martin murders, Charles Stanton had insulted the mother and father, and hinted that he had been intimate with the daughter. To avenge his sister's honor, Pete Lucero one evening rode up to the door of Stanton's store, where Stanton was sitting just inside in a chair tipped back against the counter. Lucero jerked his gun and fired at Stanton, who escaped with his life as the bullet clipped one of his ear lobes. The would-be avenger had to flee Stanton's wrath, and hid out for some months.

On the night of November 13, 1886, Stanton and a man named Kelly were in Stanton's store at a late hour, when some customers pulled up outside in the dark. Kelly heard them talking and went outside. The customers turned out to be three Mexicans, who inquired about the road to Walnut Grove and a camp site for the night. Then they asked if they could buy some tobacco. Thinking them to be strangers, Stanton told them to come in, which two of them did. As he went behind the counter to get the tobacco, Stanton turned and recognized the Mexicans as Pete and Sesto Lucero. They raised their rifles and shot Stanton three times in the breast, killing him. As he fell, he cried out, "I'm killed — blow out the light!" Kelly extinguished the lantern and ran for a side room where there were guns, but Chano Lucero took a shot at him through the window. Pete and Sesto ran outside, thinking it was Kelly shooting. In the dim light they shot and killed the man they saw. It was their brother, Chano.

The bloody career of Charles P. Stanton was over at last. There is evidence but no proof that Charles B. Genung was involved in Stanton's death. He once wrote, " . . . then commenced a terrible struggle between Stanton and his gang on one side and myself and a few Mexican placer miners on the other side, with the result that six of them including Stanton himself are sojourning in the happy hunting grounds." If he was involved, Arizona is in his debt. The villainous Francisco Vega was forced to flee for his life, and it is said he escaped into Old Mexico and never paid for his crimes. The remnants of his gang continued to operate out of Weaver, however.

A new leader of the cutthroat band emerged, called the "King of Weaver." The full extent of their activities will never be known, for they had sometimes dressed up in Indian garb and paint, swooped down on their victims with war whoops, and tried to pass off their deeds as the work of Indians. In Weaver in 1898 a respected citizen, a saloon-keeper and merchant named Segna, was murdered and a Prescott newspaper, the *Journal-Miner,* let loose an editorial blast. It called for the town to be wiped off the map, calling it "one of the darkest spots in Arizona." The editorial continued, "Weaver has reveled in its bloody misdeeds for too long. Unless courts supply a remedy soon, the place should be razed to the ground and wiped away. It is the darkest spot in

Old building in Stanton, Arizona, said to be the original store and stagecoach station owned by Charles P. Stanton. If it is, Stanton was killed inside it by the Lucero brothers.

crimes and criminals west of the Rockies and, if not obliterated, justice will be equally as guilty as the men who support and sanction its bloodcurdling existence."

But Weaver was already on its way to oblivion. Some eight or ten miles to the northwest the Congress Mine discovered by Dennis May was expanding its workings as the placers at Weaver were being worked out. Gradually the remaining miners and citizens at Weaver gravitated to the new camp at Congress, leaving the gang to its own devices and the town to its inevitable deterioration and decay. Soon after the turn of the century it was deserted except for a few hangers-on. Over the years, time has done its work, and today there is not one habitable building of the old town left, only tumbled-down ruins. There are glory holes and scraped earth, and evidence of workings in the bed of Weaver Creek, but Rich Hill now looks down only on the poor and forlorn scene of past glories.

The town of Stanton, however, did not disappear with the death of Charles Stanton. It survived as a station on the Wickenburg to Prescott stage road for some time, and others operated Charles Stanton's old store, meeting his same fate. A Frenchman named Vendier who was running it was killed there by a Mexican miner, and later on a couple named Franks was murdered there. Nine years after Stanton's death a mining engineer named George Upton bought the entire gold mining camp, built a home, and lived there many years as Stanton dwindled into a ghost town. When Upton became too old to care for himself, his niece, a former nurse named Maurine Sanborn, joined him in Arizona and cared for him for the rest of his life.

When not occupied with caring for Upton, Miss Sanborn did her best to preserve the old town and run off vandals. She once told how, during the depression, Stanton was surrounded by tents, occupied by men trying to earn a living by working the old placers. Evidently the need for funds eventually became too great, for in 1959 she sold part of the town to the "Saturday Evening Post" magazine. The magazine used it as a sales promotion, changed its name to Ulcer Gulch, and awarded it as a prize to the winner of a jingle contest. The lady who won it, a resident of New York City, had never before heard of it, nor had ever been in Arizona. She had no idea what to do with her prize and disposed of the property again.

Since then the old ghost town and the surrounding property have passed through other hands, but Stanton still survives with some of the buildings remaining. Best preserved is the old Stanton Hotel, a weather-beaten but fascinating remnant of the past. Other buildings are an old saloon and dance hall, and one said to be the actual store and stage station once occupied by Charles P. Stanton himself. Evidences of Stanton's mining heritage are all around for the visitor to view, but the old town changes little these days. Unchanged is the bright Arizona sunshine, the rugged beauty of Antelope Mountain and the surrounding hills, the sight of green lizards poking their heads up through piles of old lumber or rock crevices, and the air of tranquility that has settled once more over the desert.

Traveling northward from Wickenburg toward Prescott on U. S. Highway 89, one comes to Congress Junction and Ye Ol' Trading Post, an interesting shop of antiquities and rocks that has a little age on it, too. About a mile past it is a road sign pointing the way eastward toward Stanton. About six miles along on a well-graded dirt road the traveler finds Stanton, drowsing under the sun. A couple of miles further on, after a left turn, are Weaver Creek and what remains of the fierce old outlaw den of Weaver. Just beyond that a half-mile or so is another, more recent ghost town, Octave, where there are several private mining properties, some being worked again. They provide a footnote to our narrative — some of the claims at Octave were once owned by Charles B. Genung, the nemesis of Charles P. Stanton.

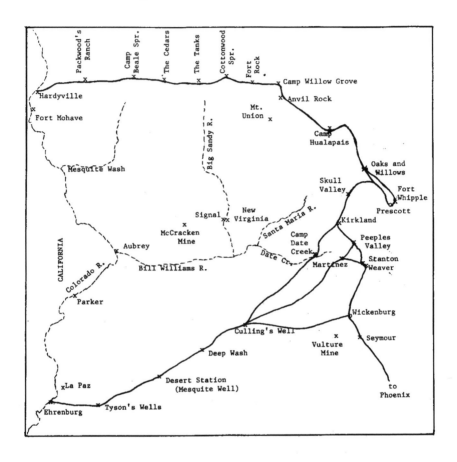

PRESCOTT TO THE COLORADO RIVER
Stagecoach and Freight Routes, c. 1863-c. 1905

CHAPTER 3
Prescott to the Colorado River

In 1864 Fort Whipple settled on Granite Creek in Arizona's Bradshaw Mountains, after having moved a couple of times and been known by other names. Since the protection of the military was a necessity, the territorial government of newly-appointed officials moved with it to Granite Creek. On its banks a new capital city which would be named Prescott was platted, and the roots of government had at last been put down. The town, fort, and inhabitants of the area had common problems, though — supply and communications with the rest of the world. In every direction there was only wilderness: mountains, canyons, deserts.

But to the west, just over a hundred miles away was the great — and navigable — Colorado River. Steamboats had been plying it for years, supplying communities along its stream and inland mines. From Prescott, trails which became roads quickly stretched out to the river ports.

All of this came about because of the momentous events in 1863 that shaped Arizona's destiny. In that year Congress established Arizona Territory separately from New Mexico Territory, of which it had been a part. In 1863 there were two expeditions of gold-seekers to Arizona's interior, both highly successful, attracting thousands of people to the area. One was commanded by Capt. Joseph Reddiford Walker, which found gold along Lynx Creek and in many other locations in the Bradshaws. The other was the Peeples expedition (see chapter on Stanton) that discovered the gold placers along Weaver Creek and on Rich Hill, some distance south of Prescott. Then, in the summer of 1863, a member of the Peeples expedition, Henry Wickenburg, discovered the fabulous Vulture gold mine. Wickenburg sold his interest in the mine and never profited from its riches, but settled on a ranch on the Hassayampa River some fifteen miles from the Vulture. There the town of Wickenburg evolved as the mine's supply and connecting point, and from the town supply trails and roads reached out toward the Colorado River ports.

Prescott, Wickenburg, Stanton and Weaver were wide-open frontier towns, and for the next forty years in the towns and along the trails to the Colorado the action was as lively as any in the saga of the West. There were fights with hostile Indians, stagecoach robberies, and even adventure on the freight runs that have a story all their own in the romance of the frontier. In the research library of the Sharlot Hall Museum in Prescott are found the reminiscences of Thomas D. Sanders, a pioneer who lived long in and around Prescott, that are fascinating revelations of that era. Sanders was a freighter, traveling the old roads many times.

The path first used from Prescott to the Colorado went northwesterly to the old Beale wagon road roughly following the thirty-fifth parallel, then west to Hardyville on the river. Capt. William Hardy, a steamer captain, laid out the route and maintained it as a toll road, to recoup his road-building costs. The stops and stations varied over the years, and differed with freighters and stagecoachers. Sanders names those he used when he first freighted over it in about 1866. First was a campground named Oaks and Willows, Willow Creek which no doubt was Willow Grove Station, a stage stop, then Fort Rock. From there it was Cottonwood Creek, the Tanks and the Cedars near today's town of Kingman, then Beale Springs and on to Hardyville.

Fort Rock was never a military post, but got its name from a desperate fight with Indians. In 1866 the mail carrier named Poindexter, bound for Prescott with an escort of three soldiers,

Office of the pioneer newspaper, the Arizona Miner, on South Montezuma Street, Prescott. (Courtesy Arizona Historical Society)

arrived at the station near Mount Union. It was kept by J. J. Buckman and his fifteen-year-old son. Outside the station the boy had outlined a play fort, a foot or so high, with rocks. The next morning when Buckman and one of the soldiers went outside the station to tend the stock, about a hundred Hualapai Indians opened fire on the station from ambush. Buckman and the soldier dived behind the rocks of the play fort, pinned down there by the Indians' fire.

Inside, the soldiers and young Thad Buckman sprang to the gun ports and began answering the Indians' shots. When their guns jammed, Poindexter and the soldiers kept loading for the boy, lifting him up to a gun port so he could continue shooting. From their positions in the front, Buckman and the soldier held off the Indians all day, and at night, tiring of the game, the Indians withdrew. The name of Fort Rock for the station was inevitable.

The well-known account of Arizona frontier life by an army officer's wife, Martha Summerhayes, published in 1908 as *Vanished Arizona*, recounts her journey over the Hardyville-Prescott road in 1874. The trip was uneventful, but she mentions a stop between Hardyville and Beale Springs named Packwood's Ranch at which there was a bar. She also mentions Anvil Rock and Camp Hualapais as campgrounds between Willow Grove Springs and Prescott. She described the usual line of march of an army column as first the troops marching in advance, then the ambulances and carriages drawn by smaller mules and carrying any dependents traveling with the army. Following this were the supply wagons pulled by six larger, stronger mules, and at the end a small rear guard. Progress was slow, the average day's journey about twenty miles.

According to Sanders' account, the first freighters out of Prescott were the Miller brothers, Sam and Jake, who had been members of the Walker party but took to ranching west of Prescott. Their first ventures were with pack trains using up to thirty burros. Demand was great, however, and with the improved roads the Miller brothers changed to six-mule teams pulling wagons. In time that increased to ten-to-twenty-mule teams hauling heavy wagons loaded with 16,000 to 20,000 and more pounds of goods, while pulling a heavily-loaded trailer wagon. There were other large outfits mentioned by Sanders: Dr. Wilson Jones could put ten ten-mule teams on the road with twenty heavy freight wagons, Creed Bryant six large ten-mule teams pulling twelve big freight wagons, and Fred Freeman boasting five ten-mule teams and ten wagons.

Sanders' was one of the smaller outfits, starting out with oxen but soon switching over to the use of mules. Ox teams cost less, $75 to $125 per yoke, and their rigging was merely a yoke and chain. Good mules cost $200 to $400 per span, and their complex harness for a ten-mule team could cost $300 and up. Mules also were faster, required less feed and could pull heavier loads. Though horses were also used, they were considered more temperamental and less hardy than mules, and were seldom used by freight outfits. Sanders and the other small freighters did most of the local and shorter-range hauling.

In 1866 while Sanders' freight outfit was in Hardyville, the Miller brothers came in from Prescott with one of their big outfits. While they were loading for the return trip, a man named Ed Bowers arrived from California driving a herd of a hundred or more cattle bound for army posts under a government contract. The family of George Banghart, a wife and four daughters, also arrived bound for the Arizona interior, and all these parties, the Millers, Bowers and Bangharts, decided to travel together.

While this was going on, the station keeper at Willow Grove Springs back along the trail, Ed Clower, had been murdered by Hualapai Indians. Sanders believed it was the work of one Indian, hired by Clower to find some strayed horses, but who then killed Clower when the opportunity arose. News traveled fast along the trail, however, and when he began his return journey or shortly thereafter, Sam Miller of the freighting brothers knew of the murder by the Indians of a man he called a friend. The Indians were showing more than a passing interest in Bowers' cattle herd, too, so Miller was more than a little incensed and apprehensive about the Hualapais as the freight wagon train and its caravan set out on the long trail toward Prescott.

As this company was pulling into Beale Springs, thirty-five miles along the road, the low hills around seemed to come alive with Hualapais. They completely surrounded the train and its encampment and made repeated efforts to stampede the cattle. While the Indians kept the outfit surrounded for two days, Miller managed to slip two couriers through their cordon, dispatched back to Hardyville for re-inforcements. Captain Hardy organized a relief party of ten freighters, including Sanders and one of his men, Jack Akin. Under Akin's command they swiftly set out for

Beale Springs, arriving at two in the morning, but too late for the drama.

The previous day the Indians had wanted to talk, and Sam Miller allowed the Hualapai chief, Wauba Yuma, and another Indian to approach the camp, reportedly with a white flag. Asked what he wanted, Wauba Yuma replied that the Hualapais wanted the whites to share those fine beef cattle with them. Sam Miller was already very angry over the murder of Clower, impatient at the two-day delay, and worried over the responsibility he felt for the safety of the Banghart family. Enraged, he pulled his gun and shot Wauba Yuma dead on the spot. Others made short work of the chief's companion. The rest of the Indians fled in all directions, as they sometimes were disposed to do if their chief met death. The caravan then resumed its journey.

After consulting with Miller, the relief party turned back toward Hardyville. It was under orders from Capt. Hardy to kill any Indians found east of a point called Union Pass, as they were then off their reservation and considered to be hostiles. The whites suspected there was an Indian camp north of Beale Springs, and slipped up on its supposed location in the night. At daybreak they crept up a ridge overlooking the camp and seeing nothing, rushed it. It was abandoned, so the party put it to the torch and continued northwesterly. At the edge of the great Sacramento Valley they discovered tracks of a small band of Indians that led out across the valley.

After following the trail for perhaps 20 miles, the pursuers saw a thin veil of smoke ascending from a little basin at the foot of Union Pass. They came upon the Indians at about the same time they were themselves seen, and the Indians tried to flee on foot. The whites were on horseback and soon had captured the hostiles. A council was then held by the white men, who decided to carry out Hardy's orders. There were eight Indians and ten white men. Akins told his men that anyone who did not want to carry out the execution should step aside, and two men did. Turning to the others, Akin said, "Now that leaves just one for each of us. You see that fellow there eating jerky with a knife? Well, I want to scalp him with his own knife."

"Each of us agreed on a victim," wrote Sanders, "and when Akins gave the command a sharp report rang out and eight Indians received a sudden introduction to the happy hunting grounds. Each man stepped up to his victim and scalped him . . .

We went through their few effects . . . and found a few good buckskins we took along with us. We burned the rest of their trinkets, and leaving their bodies to broil in the sun or furnish food for the coyotes, we returned to Hardyville to report what we had done."

Arriving at Hardyville at two in the morning, they awoke Hardy who let them into the store. "Well, Jack, what luck?" he inquired of Akin. "Pretty good," replied Akin, "but not as good as I would like to have done." He threw the scalp of his victim on the counter, and the rest of his men followed suit. Hardy counted them, looked up and said, "Well, boys, I guess I can afford to treat on that." Taking tin cups from the shelf, he dipped them one at a time in a barrel of peach brandy, and handed each man a cup full of the liquor each with a whole peach floating in it. After drinking to their successful raid, Hardy roused the cook to get them all an early breakfast.

Sanders loaded his freight outfit with government supplies for Fort Whipple, and back in Prescott took a contract to haul logs for a sawmill. Two sawmills had been built near Prescott as lumber was a commodity much in demand, and freighters could make good money on two-way hauls, taking lumber on the

Remains of historic Fort Tyson near Quartzsite, Arizona. (Courtesy Arizona Historical Society)

out-trips to their destinations, then freighting merchandise on the trip back in. As the Miller brothers were also hauling logs, they and Sanders worked together to better protect themselves and their stock from lurking Indians. "We had one herder," related Sanders, "who would let (the oxen) out of the corral at daybreak, let them feed until about eight o'clock, then yoke them up. We would work them until about four in the afternoon. He would turn them out to feed until sundown, when they were driven into the big corral for the night. This system worked magnificently for just about one month.

"One evening just before sundown the Indians jumped the oxen. Scared and surprised, the herder managed to drive three head into camp . . . The first we knew about it was when we heard the bell on the bell ox. Looking up, we saw him and two others come flying through the trees with the herder right behind them on the dead run. The Indians got away with seventeen head . . . Breaking for our cabins and getting our guns, we started in pursuit . . ." It was too late. Even after the incident was reported to Fort Whipple the next morning and troopers were sent in pursuit, none of the animals were ever recovered, nor any of the raiders caught.

Hardyville was the northermost Colorado river port at which Arizona freight was delivered, though exploring steamers did ascend the Colorado as far north as Callville, now under the waters of Lake Mead. Downstream there were numerous small landings for nearby mining camps, and an important port named La Paz. It grew there as the result of the discovery in 1862 of placer gold close by on the bank of the river, by trappers in a party guided by the redoubtable mountain man Pauline Weaver. The town sprang up so quickly that for a time as early as 1862, and until 1868, it was the seat of Yuma County. La Paz was also near the point where the Bradshaw Road from Los Angeles and Bakersfield in California crossed the river, headed for Arizona's interior. This fortunate location near the placer mines and at trade cross-traffic attracted merchants who opened stores, saloons and other businesses serving travelers on the road and river, and, by 1863, perhaps 1,500 permanent residents.

The first merchants, Hyman Mannassee and Manuel Ravena prominent among them, were soon joined by California entrepreneurs whose names would become well-known in Arizona such as Michael and Joseph Goldwater and Philip Drachman along with many others. Michael Goldwater quickly became the dominant figure in La Paz, and the Goldwaters branched out into Prescott and eventually Phoenix. The interest of these merchants in La Paz and the establishment of the Bradshaw Road soon began to draw traffic away from the northern routes from Los Angeles through Hardyville to Prescott.

Though the Bradshaw Road was easily the shortest, fastest route from Los Angeles to La Paz, it had the serious drawback of having to cross an almost waterless desert. That was never completely overcome, and a major portion of passengers and freight continued to go by water, down the California coast, around the Baja peninsula, and up the Gulf of California and the Colorado River. The amazing stories of the riverboat captains such as Hardy, Isaac Polhamus, Jack Mellon and others are a chapter in history all their own, for another time. In 1863 the needs of the mining camps at Weaver, Stanton, Wickenburg and increasingly of Prescott made a road from La Paz to the Arizona interior an immediate and vital necessity.

Early in 1864 a wagon road laid out by Herman Ehrenberg, a mining engineer, was completed into central Arizona. Since it crossed one of the most desolate of deserts, it had its problems. The all-pervading heat in summer, clouds of fine, powdery dust and almost non-existent graze for animals were bad enough, but lack of water was the worst. The stations along the line changed from time to time, as new wells were dug and new station keepers braved the heat, solitude and dangers of the desert.

In 1868, a freighter and station keeper named W. D. Fenter in the March 14th issue of the *Arizona Miner* of Prescott ran this ad: "The Safest and Best Road from the Colorado River to the Interior of Arizona. Six Wells on the Desert between La Paz and Date Creek. Abundance of water for men and animals at all times. Distances: La Paz to Tyson's Wells, 20 miles, to Desert Station 27 miles, to Granite Wash 12 miles, to Middle Station 10 miles, to Kelsey's 5 miles, to Culling's 12 miles. This leaves a short day's travel over the desert without water. The Indians are peaceable on this road."

This road divided at Culling's Well, according to the military map of 1879, which shows one branch continuing eastward toward Wickenburg 37 miles away, another to Martinez Station at Congress Junction and on to Stanton and Weaver, and a third branch toward Date Creek and on to Prescott. A story in the

Florence *Tribune* of September 7, 1895, told the story of two men who tried to alleviate that "short trip across the desert without water" from Culling's well to Martinez Station by trying to dig a well and establish a station of their own. It was said to have been written by the "Father of Arizona" himself, Charles D. Poston, and appeared first in a California newspaper. " . . . I recently unearthed the history of one of these wells," wrote Poston. " . . . It was abandoned and now is nothing but a half-covered shaft with a lonely grave beside it." The military map of 1879 shows this spot as King's Well.

"(At a date unknown) Dave King and one Dan, surname unknown, started out for Wickenburg on the Hassayampa River to try their luck digging a well on the La Paz road. . . . Could they succeed in striking water at some point thirty or forty miles from Wickenburg there would be easy times ahead. They selected a point some thirty-five miles out on the desert as a favorable location for a water station, and when the wagon that had brought them unloaded their tools and camp outfit and (turned back, it) left them there alone. (They) went to work and cleared away the cactus and greasewood to make a good place on which to spread their blankets and build their campfire. A six-shooter apiece, a few blankets, two picks and a shovel, a frying pan and coffee pot and some flour, bacon and beans was the extent of their capital, but they knew the future would turn out all right . . ."

Two months later they had sunk their shaft to over 100 feet, and were beginning to think they ought to be getting pretty close to water. One day they stopped for lunch, and while they were eating, two sulky-looking Mexicans approached from the road and, without ceremony, were invited to sit down and help themselves. The two partners noticed that the Mexicans wore uniforms and carried army muskets, and decided they were evidently deserters from a company of Mexican soldiers stationed at the time near Prescott. No questions were asked, however, that being considered impolite on the frontier. Dave and Dan finished eating and went back to work, telling their guests to help themselves and eat all they wanted.

After finishing eating, the Mexicans took their guns and sneaked up on the shaft where their hosts were working, about a hundred yards away from the camp. Dave was at the bottom of the shaft, getting ready to fill the bucket, and Dan at the top looking down in ready to let down the windlass. A later examination of their tracks showed the Mexicans stopped about half-way, and one of them put a bullet through Dan's back. Dan threw up his hands and fell headlong into the shaft. The Mexicans crept up to the rim and peered down inside. Hearing and seeing nothing, they rifled the camp and fled to the Hassayampa River and down it to the Gila River.

At the bottom of the shaft, Dave heard the gunshot, and saw the body of Dan come hurtling downward toward him. In the instant he had, Dave squeezed his body into a corner of the square shaft. The falling body missed him, landing with a tremendous thud. Dave remained motionless, fearing what was to come next, but when the murderers could not see or hear him on looking down the shaft, Dave was left at the bottom with the body of his dead partner. He realized there was very little hope for rescue; the well-site was a quarter-mile from the sparsely traveled road, but his prayer for a miracle was answered.

Johnny Duff, the mail carrier between Wickenburg and La Paz, passed along the road by King's camp about two-thirty in the afternoon. Seeing neither of the partners around, he decided to

Goldwater's general merchandise store on South Cortez Street, Prescott.
(Courtesy Arizona Historical Society)

investigate. Looking into the well shaft, he shouted, "Hello down there!" Recognizing the voice, Dave yelled, "Is that you, Johnny? For God's sake haul me out! There's a dead man down here." No sooner said than done. Johnny continued on his way, and Dave began walking toward Wickenburg. He arrived early next morning, and soon a party started back to the well to give poor Dan a Christian burial, in the manner of the brotherhood of men on the frontier.

Leaving others to bury Dan, freighter Creed Bryant and Joe Blackwell mounted up and started for the Hassayampa River. At a well-known crossing they picked up the tracks of the two murderers and followed them to the wagon road, the shortest distance to Old Mexico. When the pursuers found the two muskets which the Mexicans had thrown away to lighten their load, they were certain they were on the right trail. On they pushed, taking several short cuts, until at sunset they reached the banks of the flowing Salt River. They knew that they had arrived before the Mexicans who were afoot, and planned to capture the murderers at the crossing.

As they slept and kept watch by turns, Bryant during the night heard splashing, and watched the two Mexicans wade the river. At daylight Bryant and Blackwell took up the trail and in the distance saw their quarry fishing in the river. Taking advantage of the cover of trees along the river, they sneaked up on the men and soon had captured them. Questioned why they murdered the man at the well, the Mexicans were silent until one finally admitted their fear that they would be followed and caught as deserters. Bryant and Blackwell then gave them a choice — the hangman's noose or a rifle bullet. They chose bullets. Bryant and Blackwell executed them forthwith, retrieved the six-shooters they had stolen, and returned to Wickenburg where Dave King was waiting to hear that Dan's murder had been avenged.

The Colorado was still a wild river then, not yet curbed by the dams that would be built, and not infrequently when high water subsided the river had changed its course. That caprice of fate doomed the town of La Paz, for when the river changed course it left La Paz high and dry — and inland. "About the last of 1866," says the reminiscences of Mr. Sanders, "after the river had changed its course at La Paz it became necessary to build another river port to receive goods and so the Goldwater people started the town of Ehrenberg about five or six miles down the Colorado River from where La Paz stood . . . The place was named for Herman Ehrenberg, a mining engineer and pioneer in the great Southwest. Up to that same year, 1866, Mr. Ehrenberg lived at La Paz and was found murdered as he was en route for San Bernardino alone. No one ever knew why he was killed, but it was attributed to Indians." Other sources say Ehrenberg was carrying $3,500 when he stopped at the Dos Palmas station for the night. During the night he was shot and killed, and robbed. No one was ever apprehended as his murderer or charged with the deed.

"At Ehrenberg, Mike Goldwater had a small wharf built," continued Sanders, " (with) store houses and a few other necessary buildings put up. Several Mexican families took up their abode there and it was much the same kind of settlement as La Paz. Goldwater then turned his attention to putting in a series of wells to afford watering places and stations along the route from Ehrenberg to Prescott. From Prescott south in the order in which we would come to them, they were Skull Valley, Kirkland, Willow Springs, Martinez (Station) now known as Congress Junction, Culling's Well, Deep Wash, Mesquite Well, and Tyson's Well . . . There was a house at each one of the places mentioned and charges were made for watering stock for each head night and morning, twenty-five cents, and fifty cents per barrel for every one that was hauled away.

"The wells were dug at considerable hazard to life . . . Ordinary miners without timbering or anything would sink a well from forty to three hundred feet and trust to a burro or mule operating a whim to pull up the dirt. Culling's Well was the deepest of them all and was sunk to a depth of 300 feet. Desert Well became a close second with a depth of 250 feet, and the wells at Deep Wash, Mesquite Well and Tyson's were each eighty feet deep. The shallowest was at Tyson's and was forty feet in depth. In all of them what water there was, was down nearly the whole depth of the well . . . (They) were sometimes cased near the surface with heavy planking or timbers, but that was all. The water was brought out by means of a whim . . . The motive power would be either a burro, a mule or a horse. They had the traveler at all those places. It was a case of no pay, no drink when it came to watering stock. Of course, no one ever thought of making a charge for drinking water."

The first three stations mentioned by Sanders, Skull Valley, Kirkland and Willow Springs, were in ranch country southwest of Prescott. There were ranches all around the Skull Valley Station, Kirkland Station was at Bill Kirkland's ranch and Willow Springs at the ranch of J. D. Monihon on Willow Creek. Both Kirkland and Monihon were prominent among Arizona pioneers. Despite the establishment of Camp Date Creek (first called Camp McPherson) south of Prescott, on Date Creek, to protect traffic on the road to La Paz from attacks by Yavapai Indians as well as far-ranging bands of Mohaves and Hualapais, the Indians continued their old habits right under the noses of the military. Sanders had been traveling with other freight outfits for mutual protection, but, he wrote, "the Indians were jumping outfits, stealing stock, and now and then killing someone. We who had been traveling together seemed to be playing in luck as Miller's outfit had been jumped, but the skirmish that followed did not amount to much, as there were plenty of men in the train to stand the redskins off . . . Doc Jones' outfit was jumped at The Sinks of Date Creek and a hard battle ensued. Dutch Henry, who had come from California with Jake Miller and me, was slain in that battle. Several mules were wounded and after a desperate time of it the Indians were bested after making vain attempts to take the entire outfit . . . It was said there was not less than seventy-five of them . . .

"That same year Fred Freeman was jumped at Skull Valley with his six ten-mule teams. He had pitched camp about four o'clock in the afternoon. He no sooner had his animals unhooked from the wagons until 18 or 20 Indians came running along low ridges close to and overlooking the camp. When in easy range, they hoisted a white flag and bravely walked into camp. They carried a lot of buckskin with them and pretended they wanted to trade for coffee and sugar. They were about to get away with their stall when one of Freeman's teamsters happened to notice one Indian bearing a knife hidden up his sleeve. Upon closely watching some others, he saw that there were several who carried knives in the same way, and that the Indians were going to attack them. Freeman was busy with his palaver with the Indians when in a low tone the teamster told Freeman the Indians carried knives. Without any display of suspicion, Freeman said very calmly, "Boys, get your guns," and with that instantly every man in camp jumped for his gun. The Indians bounded out of camp like a bunch of scared deer and ran headlong in all directions. The teamsters were all good marksmen and succeeded in killing all but three or four of the renegades . . ."

Culling's Well, the first station on the desert, has a fabulous history all its own. The owner was Charles C. Culling, whose name in many accounts is corrupted to Cullen or Cullin. Born in London, England, Culling arrived in Arizona in the early 1860's and worked at the Vulture mine. After some prospecting ventures, he decided to try to establish a stage station, and dug a well that never struck water. He moved five miles west, and at a great depth (reports are that it was 240 to 300 feet deep) struck an inexhaustible supply of pure, sweet water. There he built his station that lasted as long as the desert road was in use.

Culling was a kindly man, who in 1871 married a 14-year-old girl, Maria Valenzuela, in Wickenburg. They had three sons, Daniel, Charles, and Albert. Culling ran cattle on the desert around the station, which of course the Apaches stole on occasion. On one of these raids, later recalled by his son Charles, the Indians burned several stacks of hay and ran off a large herd of cattle and horses. Culling with some others pursued the raiders eastward, enlisting the aid of soldiers at Fort McDowell. According to the *Arizona Miner* of February 2, 1871, soldiers under Lt. Ross, with Culling and his men, caught up with the Apaches, killed two of them in a fight, and recovered all the animals.

When Culling died in 1878, he was buried at the station and the *Arizona Enterprise* of Prescott said " . . . he was long and favorably known to travelers and residents in this territory. He was a good, whole-souled, jovial man, and his hearty welcome and pleasantness will be missed . . ." The *Arizona Miner* of Prescott said "Mr. Culling was one of Arizona's oldest and best citizens. He settled where he died . . . at Culling's Station, where the weary were always welcomed and found rest, the hungry (whether accompanied by plenty or the needful or otherwise) food. There is not a person who ever knew Charley Culling but will mourn his loss." Some time later his widow married Joe Drew, who had been a merchant at the Vulture Mine, and Drew took charge of the station.

The stagecoaches passed the station daily, going each way,

along with numerous freight outfits and other casual traffic. In summer the heat made all travel almost unbearable by its unrelenting intensity. Many, many travelers caught short of water perished in the desert, the road was dotted with graves along it of those unfortunates whose bodies were found and buried by subsequent passers-by. Near Cullings' two miners died by the roadside in sight of the station, and a prospector's body was found two years later only a few hundred yards from the station. Not long thereafter, just after nightfall, a youth staggered to the watering trough near the station. Almost dead from thirst, he had lain down to die on the desert when he saw the lamplight in the station's window. Somehow he found the strength to make it to the well, saving his life.

After this incident, Joe Drew began a practice that gave the station the nickname of "The Lighthouse in the Desert." Atop the station he nailed a long board, and above the board on a long pole every night swung a lighted lantern. This beacon of light, the only one in the unrelieved stillness and dark of the vast desert, beckoned to anyone lost and suffering from lack of water to the station and its life-saving well. This practice was continued every night until about 1905 when a new road bypassed the old station and it was abandoned.

Very little is known about the temporary stations along the

Typical 20-mule freight outfit, hauling heavily-loaded freight wagon and two trailer wagons. This one is standing in front of the famous Joe Collingwood Store on Main Street, Florence. (Courtesy Arizona Historical Society)

trail, or the two permanent ones at Desert Well and Mesquite Well. More is known about Tyson's Wells or Fort Tyson, twenty miles east of Ehrenberg, established by and subsequently owned by men prominent in territorial history whose stories are better preserved. Two of these were Charles and Joseph Tyson. Joseph was superintendent of a mine in the Plomosa Mountains. When he and business associates in La Paz were anxious to get the freight road opened to the interior in 1864, Joe Tyson undertook having a station and well established twenty miles east of the Colorado.

At a desert wash where water was known to be, because of wells called Los Pozos (Spanish for "Wells") a couple of miles up the wash, Charles Tyson sank a shaft and struck water at only 40 feet. There Tyson built a stage station and dug other wells, and of course it became known as Tyson's Wells. It was also called Fort Tyson because other dwellers in the area, fearing raids by the Mohaves in the vicinity, built a fort-like structure as defense against the expected attacks. There is no evidence that the Mohaves ever attacked it directly, but the travelers on the desert road were fair game for the Indians and bandits for attack and robbery. Though thousands of travelers passed by and hundreds of freight outfits rumbled along the road, few settlers made homes there because of the desolation and summer heat.

In 1868, A. H. Peeples of Wickenburg, organizer of the Peeples expedition in 1863 and once resident of Peeples Valley (see chapter on Stanton), bought the station and turned it over to George Roberts to run. Roberts, who had come with Peeples from the California gold fields, lived there with his wife and four children for a time. Subsequently it was owned by James McMullen, who sold it to Mike Welz in 1879. Welz stayed a while, for he was the postmaster when the first post office opened under the name "Tyson's" in 1893. However, it closed again two years later. The celebrated Arizona pioneer Charles Genung also ran a saloon there about 1900.

Though the desert road and its wells and station were maintained for more than forty years, almost nothing of their history has been preserved. The desolation, unrelenting heat, dust and isolation discouraged settlement and made them lonely outposts for the station keepers. Martha Summerhayes, the officer's wife, traveled the road from Prescott to Ehrenberg in

1875, and in *Vanished Arizona* described the trip over the vast emptiness of the desert. Her first two days as they passed the ranch stations were pleasant because great quantities of milk to drink were available. The third day she arrived at Culling's Well, where Culling's wife put Summerhayes' infant to bed in the crib of her own child, Daniel, to the extreme gratitude of Mrs. Summerhayes.

The next day they set out on the desert. "It seemed so white, so bare, so endless," she wrote, "and so still; irreclaimable, eternal, like Death itself. The stillness was appalling." Of their stop at Mesquite Wells, she wrote, "A Mexican worked the (well) machinery with the aid of a mule . . . The man dwelt alone in his desolation, with no living being except his mule for company. How could he endure it! I was not able even faintly to comprehend it . . . He occupied a small hut, and there he stayed, year in and year out, selling water to passing travelers. The thought of the hermit and his dreary surroundings filled my mind for a long time after we drove away . . ."

Mrs. Summerhayes' party stopped for the night at Desert Station, at a "good ranch kept by Hunt and Dudley, Englishmen, I believe . . . Their place was clean and attractive, which was more than could be said of the place where we stopped the next night, a place called Tyson's Wells. We slept in our tent that night, for of all places on earth a poorly kept ranch in Arizona is the most melancholy and uninviting. It reeks of everything unclean, morally and physically."

At the road's Colorado River stop, Ehrenberg had its day as the successor to La Paz, junction of the river traffic and the road from California to the Arizona interior. On October 2, 1869, the *Arizona Miner* of Prescott said that "The place (Ehrenberg) is growing with amazing force. The new warehouse built by Goldwater is 75 x 150 feet. J. B. Tuttle has completed a large building for wagon and blacksmith shops. Tom Goodman has a hotel, Jack Schwartz a billiard hall, and many private buildings going up. Steamboats are arriving regularly and trade with the interior is good."

The Tom Goodman who built the hotel was one of the bad guys, though. He brought a new bride to the town, and later for some reason brutally murdered her. He drowned her by throwing her into the river, and when she grabbed a tree branch to try to save herself, he beat upon her hands until she was forced to release her grasp and slip under the water. No one knows why he was never brought to justice for this crime. Instead, he was offered the job as postmaster, but declined. It was then given to one Jesus Daniels, who apparently did not understand his duties. He never bought any stamps, never delivered any mail nor got in touch with his superiors. When a postal inspector made inquiry, he found over 200 undelivered letters. Included was an official one, unopened, from Postmaster General John Wannamaker. In it he thanked Daniels for the efficient conduct of his post office.

The end of the desert road, its colorful stage stations with their life-saving wells, and the western romance of the stagecoach and the freight wagon train was in sight when the Santa Fe railroad began building across the desert in 1904. Then a new highway was built roughly alongside the tracks, and the desert trail was no more. The town of Quartzsite is preserving old Fort Tyson as an historic monument. A few miles west of Aguila in the McMullen Valley are the remains of the ruined adobes and other wreckage of Culling's Well station, with a little cemetery nearby where Culling sleeps among the unfortunate desert travelers who never reached his well. It was used for a time by cattle and sheep outfits, but now is caved-in and abandoned. Off on some desert side road, abandoned and forgotten also, restored to the deep stillness and pitch-black darkness of nights broken only by the moon and stars are the forlorn remains of Desert Station and Mesquite Well.

Can anyone visit these historic spots today, where the thousands, human and beast, passed by? U. S. Highway 60 from Wickenburg to Brenda approximates it now. Five or six miles north of the location known as Gladden is the site of Culling's Well. Somewhere in the desert south of the highway you may be able to find Desert Station and Mesquite Well, long ago forgotten by an uncaring New West, where if it doesn't make money, it's no good. But in the winter or spring, go out to the desert, find an old timer and inquire. He may be able to help you. But hurry — they, like the Old West, are fading fast, and soon they all will be gone.

CHAPTER 4

An Arizona Adventure in 1864

On December 5, 1863, a journalist well-known and well-traveled in his day left his home in Oakland, California, in the morning, to travel across the bay to San Francisco on various business matters. His name was J. Ross Browne. En route from one stop to another, he ran into an old friend from his days in Washington, D. C., where he had been employed. The friend's name was Charles D. Poston, known in history as the "Father of Arizona." While renewing their friendship, Poston told Browne that, on that very afternoon at four o'clock, he was leaving for Arizona on the steamer "Senator" from San Francisco harbor. The upshot of this conversation was that Poston invited Browne to accompany him on his trip to Arizona. All arrangements had already been made; Browne merely had to be at the dock on time.

Browne hurried back to Oakland, packed a knapsack with a few shirts, pipe, tobacco, and a few pencils and paints as he was also an illustrator, bade goodbye to his wife and children, and was on the steamer when it left the dock. His host, Poston, was an extraordinary man. In 1856, he with a partner, Major Samuel P. Heintzelman, had established the Sonora Exploring and Mining Company at Tubac, Arizona, where they worked rich silver mines. With the outbreak of the Civil War in 1861, the mines had to be abandoned when troops were withdrawn from the territory to fight in that great war, leaving it to the depredations of the feared and despised Apaches. Poston had journeyed to the nation's capital, where he lobbied to have Arizona separated from New Mexico Territory, of which it had been a part. The bill making Arizona a separate territory had passed Congress on February 23, 1863.

Poston, the newly-appointed Superintendent of Indian Affairs for Arizona, had traveled overland to San Francisco, where as a government official he arranged transportation and a military escort back to the scene of his new duties. Also in Poston's party was Ammi White, Indian trader and agent for the Gila River Indian Reservation, inhabited by Pima and Maricopa Indians along the Gila River. With White were the chief of the Pimas, Antonio Azul and his interpreter named Francisco, whom White had taken to San Francisco for a visit. Everything about the trip

— the city, the people, the steamship — all was far beyond the comprehension of the primitive Pimas, who spent many days trying to explain it all to their people upon their return to the reservation.

The steamer took them to the port at San Pedro, California, where Poston's party got off. It was close by Fort Drum, at which Union army establishment they were outfitted with a military ambulance as a conveyance, mules, rations, and a six-man military escort for the trip to Arizona. Along the way, they would shoot game and pick up more rations to maintain the larder. Their route would be along the old Butterfield Overland trail, which had been abandoned by the Butterfield company at the outbreak of the war, but was still the only overland trail across southern Arizona.

Reaching the Colorado River at Fort Yuma, then on the California side, they had their first glimpse of Arizona and had no trouble crossing into it, as the river was at a very low ebb. Following the old emigrant trail along the Gila River, they came to the scene of Arizona's first gold rush, the placers at Gila City. The gold rush had been a quick boom and bust; practically nothing was left. Browne's description of the boom is famous in Arizona history.

"Rumors of extraordinary discoveries flew on the wings of the wind in every direction," he wrote. "Enterprising men hurried to the spot with barrels of whiskey and billiard tables; Jews came with ready-made clothing and fancy wares; traders crowded in with wagon-loads of pork and beans; and gamblers came with cards and monte-tables. There was everything in Gila City within a few months but a church and a jail, both of which were accounted barbarisms by the mass of the population." Gila City, however, collapsed in the space of a week. "At the time of our visit," wrote Browne, "it consisted of three chimneys and a coyote."

Fourteen miles further along, they stopped at the old Butterfield station known as Mission Camp. Here they shot some quail for dinner, and Browne made some sketches of a distinctive mountain. In another fifteen miles they reached the station at Antelope Peak, where there was good water, and where they found two soldiers stationed as a hay camp. Their next camp was at the old Butterfield stop, Grinnell's Station.

While the rest of the party continued along the trail from this point, Poston, Browne, and White took a side trip across the Gila

Antelope Peak Station on the old Butterfield trail. The Poston-Browne party camped here in 1864. (Courtesy Arizona Historical Society)

River to the Agua Caliente Ranch. Here at the site of a former Indian village was a hot spring and the ranch headquarters. It was owned by a famous early Arizonan and friend of Poston and White, King S. Woolsey. Woolsey was absent, but they were entertained by his partner, George Martin. Of the baths at the hot spring, Browne wrote "I consider them the equal of Damascus, or any other in the world."

Poston, Browne, and White rejoined their party at the next stop on the trail, Oatman Flat. The site of this station had been the scene, in 1851, of the murder of the emigrant Oatman family by renegade Yavapai Indians. There have been many accounts of the tragic waylaying of this family, and the carrying off into slavery of two young girls, Olive and Mary Ann. Here they found the grave of the Oatman family, and Browne devoted an entire chapter of his subsequent account of his travels to their story. Here also Antonio Azul and Francisco were met by members of their tribe, who had come out to greet them. There was general rejoicing, as there had been rumors among the Pimas that the two men had met with foul play. That in turn had led to some muttered threats against some Americans living on the reservation.

Beyond Oatman Flat a few miles the travelers inspected a rocky outcropping covered with petroglyphs. These are even today a curiosity to visitors to the area, where the rocks are protected by a fence. It was then called Painted Rocks, and, wrote Browne, "Mr. Poston's opinion is — and I am disposed to coincide with him — that these paintings are the records of treaties made at different times between the Indians of the Gila and those of the Colorado."

Continuing eastward, Poston's party reached the watering spot known as Maricopa Wells, at the junction of the Santa Cruz River with the Gila. Known and appreciated by all travelers along the trail for its abundance of surface water, Maricopa Wells had no facilities. The great stagecoach station and trading post of later years was still to be built. There was, however, a battleground on which the bodies of seventy-two Yuma Indians still mouldered, slain in a pitched battle between the Yumas on one side, and the Pimas and Maricopa Indians on the other, from which only three Yumas escaped.

Passing Pima Butte on the way to the Pima villages, the travelers beheld a savage and startling spectacle. "Looming up on the side of the hill, in bold outline against the sky, stood a rude cross upon which hung the dried body of an Apache, crucified about two years ago by the Maricopas," wrote Mr. Browne. "The legs and arms were fastened by cords, and the head hung forward, showing a few tufts of long hair swinging about the face. It was a strange and ghastly sight. The Maricopas do not profess the Christian faith, but this much they had learned from the missionaries who had attempted their conversion, the crucifixion was a species of torture practiced by the whites." They had punished their captive enemy in this fashion as a warning to others not to approach their villages again.

The first of the Pima villages they came to was Casa Blanca, which still exists today, where they reached the trading post and flour mill owned by Ammi White. Poston's party stayed several days, in the course of which they inspected the miles of hand-dug irrigation ditches, from which the Pimas watered their crops for miles along the Gila River. Browne stated that there were ten Pima and two Maricopa villages, with a total of about 6,000 Indians. He had high praise for their industry and their friendship with white travelers, adding that without their friendship it would be impossible to travel from Tucson to the Colorado River.

At the village of Sacaton, which was and still remains the Pimas' principal habitation, a party of thirty people was organized

Grave of the Oatman family and monument, Oatman Flat. In the background is part of the original Butterfield Trail and Cooke's Wagon Road. Browne followed the same route at this point. (Courtesy Arizona Historical Society)

to visit what they called the "Casas Grandes," (big houses), an Indian ruin on the Gila twenty miles to the southeast. Today, it is preserved as Casa Grande National Monument.

"The remains of three large edifices are distinctly visible," wrote Browne, "one of which is in a remarkable state of preservation, considering its great antiquity and the materials of which its walls are composed." Browne described all the ruined adobe or earth structures in great detail, including the main one which they judged to have been about four stories high when first built. They were already ruins when first visited by white men in 1694. "I saw no hieroglyphics in the building except the names of some Texas adventurers, and California Volunteers, scribbled with a piece of charcoal," said Browne. " . . . One name was especially worthy of note — that of Paul Weaver, 1833, a famous trapper and pioneer whose history is closely identified with that of Arizona." This name is still visible in the ruin, that of Pauline Weaver. At the very moment Browne visited the place, Weaver was occupied as guide and scout for the famed Peeples Expedition into central Arizona, which found gold at Rich Hill (see chapter on Stanton).

Before leaving the Pima villages, the party conducted a grand "pow-wow" at Sacaton with Antonio Azul and Francisco, and with the Pimas from the reservation around. Almost all the tribe must have attended, and Poston passed out trade goods as presents randomly. But when Poston's cook attempted to barter for a couple of pumpkins, he found that all of the generosity was flowing one way. Unable to get his pumpkins for a reasonable price, he ordered the pumpkin-traders out of camp. Still, the men were in the mood for pumpkin, so the trading was finally left to Poston himself.

"I left it all to Poston," wrote Browne, "whom I knew had a high order of genius for trade. He traded for two hours; he was calm and violent by turns; he reasoned and raved alternately. I fell asleep. When I awoke, triumph sat perched upon his brow. The Indians were gone. Success had crowned his efforts. Two pumpkins, the spoils of victory, lay at his feet. 'What did they cost?' was my natural inquiry. He looked a little confused, but quickly rallied and replied, 'Oh, not much for this country! Let me see — five, ten, eighteen, twenty-two. Only about twenty-two dollars in trade.' It was gratifying in all events to know that the Pimas were rapidly becoming a civilized people. Under these circumstances we thought it advisable to pursue our journey without further waste of time."

From the Pima villages, Poston's party crossed the Ninety-mile Desert toward Tucson, pausing to camp at the well where once was the Blue Water station of the Butterfield Overland route. From there it proceeded to a dry camp at Picacho Peak. The peak, a familiar landmark to today's traveler between Phoenix and Tucson on Interstate 10, did not impress Browne. "The name is Spanish and signifies 'point' or 'peak', " he wrote. "Some travelers have discovered in this curious formation of rocks some resemblance to an axe-head. There are many picachos throughout Arizona. I have been unable to see in any of them the most remote resemblance to an axe-head."

If the Picacho Peak did not impress Browne, the town of Tucson must have been a raging disappointment. Their path took them past the Point of Mountain station, then headed for the only town in the territory at that time save for the budding mining camps and Colorado River ports, all very small. Tucson had been established by the Spanish in 1776, almost a hundred years previously. Though prepared to be surprised, Browne was more than that. His description of Tucson is a classic.

"(The traveler finds) the most wonderful scatteration of human habitations his mind has ever beheld," he wrote, "a city of mud-boxes, dingy and dilapidated, cracked and baked into a composite of dust and filth; littered about with broken corrals, sheds, bake-ovens, carcasses of dead animals, and broken pottery; barren of verdure, parched, naked, and grimly desolate in the glare of the southern sun. Adobe walls without whitewash inside or out, hard earth-floors, baked and dried Mexicans, sorebacked burros, coyote dogs, and terra-cotta children; soldiers, teamsters, and honest miners lounging about the mescal shops, soaked with fiery poison; a noisy band of Sonorian buffoons, dressed in theatrical costume, cutting their antics in the public places to the most diabolical din of fiddles and guitars ever heard; a long train of government wagons preparing to start for Fort Yuma or the Rio Grande — these are what the traveler sees, and a great many things more, but in vain he looks for a hotel or lodging-house.

"The best accommodations he can possibly expect are the dried mud walls of some unoccupied outhouse, with a mud floor for his bed; his own food to eat and his own cook to prepare it; and lucky he is to possess such luxuries as these. I heard of a blacksmith named Burke, who invited a friend to stop awhile with him at Tucson. Both parties drank whiskey all day for occupation and pleasure. When bedtime came, Burke said, "Let's go home and turn in." He led the way to the Plaza, and began to hand off his clothes. "What are you doing?" inquired his guest. "Going to bed," said Burke. "This is where I gen'rally sleep." And they both turned in on the Plaza, which if hard was at least well-aired and roomy. The stranger started for the Rio Grande the next day."

The Poston-Browne party did not stay long in Tucson, using the time to re-provision and re-furbish to continue their trip which would be southward past Poston's old mining venture at Tubac, on into Sonora, then back into Arizona via a circuitous route and to Tucson before Browne returned to California. Since the country was wild and uninhabited, in full control of the barbaric and merciless Apaches in the absence of any military posts or forts, any travel had to be in force with a company of armed men or soldiers assigned to duty. Holding Tucson against the savages was a command of Union soldiers of the California Column. Thirty of them were assigned as escort to Poston's party, under a Lieutenant Arnold. "I must be permitted to say," observed Browne, "that the best view of Tucson is the rear view on the road

Tubac, 1864, from a sketch by J. Ross Browne in his book Adventures in the Apache Country. (Courtesy Arizona Historical Society)

to Fort Yuma . . . On the 19th of January (1865) we set forth on our journey . . . I may be here allowed to say that a better set of (soldiers) I never traveled with. They were good-humored, obliging, sober, and not one of them stole a pig or chicken during the entire trip."

Departing Tucson southward along the Santa Cruz River, the travelers passed the beautiful San Xavier mission, built in the eighteenth century, at the Papago village of Bac. Browne described it in glowing terms, terming its architecture as satisfying to the eye from any angle. Passing the mission and continuing along the Santa Cruz, the party was sobered by reports heard in Tucon of the murder by Apaches of two mining officials near the Mexican border, and an assault upon a third. Declared Browne, "I saw on the road between San Xavier and Tubac, a distance of forty miles, almost as many of the graves of the white men murdered by the Apaches within the past few years. Literally the roadside was marked with the burial places of these unfortunate settlers." Despite the beauty of the scenery, they were unable to enjoy it as they passed ranch after ranch burned, destroyed and desolated.

The fight against an Apache band by a lone rancher, named by Browne as Bill Rhodes and termed "one of the standard incidents in the history of Arizona," he described at length. Browne's party camped at the site of Rhodes' ranch. The rancher had returned to his house to find all his comrades killed, and himself surrounded by the Indians. Rhodes managed to break through their cordon on his horse, but the beast soon tired, and the rancher was encircled in a willow thicket. For three hours he held them off with his revolver, under continuous fire from bullets and arrows. A bullet struck him in the elbow, but he buried it in the sand to stem the flow of blood and continued fighting. When the Apaches rushed him he had only two cartridges left. He killed the Indian in the lead, halting the rest, who offered to spare his life after such a brave stand if he would surrender. Rhodes refused in no uncertain terms, whereupon the Indians held a talk, then withdrew from the field of battle.

At Tubac, former headquarters of Poston's mining company, once again they found only desolation and ruin. In the 1700's when Spain ruled the land, Tubac had been an important presidio, garrisoned by soldiers and surrounded by the farms of colonists. Abandoned and deserted, Tubac had been taken over by Poston's company in 1856 and rebuilt. But now all that had been accomplished had again been reversed. What the Apaches had not vandalized or burned, Mexicans had taken away for use in their mines below the border, now only a short distance away. A boiler, weighting 6,000 pounds, "lay on the Sonora road a little beyond Calabasas. Some Mexicans were hauling it away when they were attacked by a band of Apaches, who killed two of the party, took the teams, burned the wagon, and left the boiler on the roadside, where it lay when we passed."

There being nothing left at Tubac, the Poston-Browne party pressed on, pausing three miles down the road at the ruins of the old Tumacacori mission. Even in its desertion the beauty of the architecture and setting of the building were evident, and still is today in its present state of partial restoration as a national monument. The travelers next came to Calabasas, described by Browne as the ranch of the once governor of Sonora, Mexico, Senor Manuel Gandara. Calabasas had also been a military outpost of Mexico, then of the United States in later years. For a long time it was a ghost town, and now is under the fourteenth green of the golf course at a development known as Rio Rico, a short distance from Nogales. Browne described a previous meeting with Gandara and declared him to be only the impoverished shell of the grandee he once was, before his overthrow by the rebel Ignacio Pesqueira.

Passing Nogales (meaning "walnut") they stopped only to inspect the international boundary marker. There were no cities of Nogales that straddle the border as they do today. The boundary marker had been vandalized by Mexicans still angry and resentful at the transfer of territory which once was theirs to the United States as a result of the Gadsden Purchase. It was necessary for Poston's party to enter Mexico to re-stock their provisions at the only town of any size, Magdalena. As they traveled, Browne noted the miserable poverty in which the peasants lived, even in villages such as Imuriz, Terrenate and San Ignatio. There had been a severe drought, lasting for many years, so there had been no crops. The Apaches had stolen all the cattle, leaving nothing for the peasants at all, not even hope for the future.

The Poston-Browne party had not yet reached Magdalena when they were met by an official of the town. He stated that news of a party of Americans including thirty in military uniforms crossing into Mexico territory had reached the governor, Pesquiera. The governor was anxious to learn the nature of this unusual intrusion by armed men into a foreign state, and had instructed the official to make a close inquiry. The Americans explained that, because of the Apaches, it was necessary to travel with an armed force, and their only reason for entry to Mexico was to obtain supplies. Satisfied, the official allowed them to proceed, and at Magdalena, a town of about 1,500, they replenished their supplies.

Returning to the United States by a different route, the travelers passed by the village of Santa Cruz, where Browne interviewed a lady who had been the victim of Apache barbarism some years previously. Traveling with her family through Cocospero Canyon, a mountain pass frequently the scene of Apache ambushes, all were attacked and killed except the young woman, Dona Inez. She was carried away into slavery by the Indians, and held for about fifteen months. The international boundary was being surveyed at the time, and the incident came to the attention of Lieutenant Bartlett, in charge of the American contingent.

The famed Casa Grande ruins, visited by the Poston-Browne party in 1864. The site is now a national monument, with a protective canopy erected by the government.

Bartlett made a demand upon the Apache chief, Mangas Coloradas, in whose band she was being held, for her release. The chief insolently replied that it was none of Bartlett's business, but a matter between the Apaches and the Mexicans. Bartlett replied that, as part of the treaty with Mexico, the United States was bound to assist the Mexicans in suppressing Indian hostilities, and that if he did not produce the girl she would be rescued by force. Thereupon Mangas Coloradas turned the captive over to the Americans, and the girl, then about fifteen, was delivered to the house of the Mexican governor, at Tubac. The governor, Senor Gomez, fell in love with the girl, and she lived at his house for some time, though he already had a wife in Mexico City. At length, however, she married and moved with her husband to Santa Cruz. When interviewed by Browne, she was in her mid-twenties, and Browne stated that her beauty was fading because of illness. She spoke very kindly of her rescuer, Lieut. Bartlett, but was very reticent to talk of her time as an Apache slave.

Crossing the border into the United States, the Americans were at or near the spot which tradition says is the entry of Father Kino two centuries earlier. Once known as La Noria, it is now called

Lochiel. Poston's party was en route to the Mowry Mine, about fifteen miles from the Mexican village of Santa Cruz. Upon passing a small mining camp occupied by a Mr. Yerkes, they heard the story of the fate of the two men killed by Apaches only a few days before. J. B. Mills, superintendent of the Mowry Mine, was preparing to leave and in doing so was turning over his duties to his replacement, Edwin Stevens. Mills was escorting Stevens from Santa Cruz to the mine, when about halfway between these points they were surprised by Apaches. Stevens was killed at the first burst, but Mills put up a desperate fight before he was shot to death. The bodies were robbed, stripped and mutilated. When Poston's party reached the Mowry Mine, they found the fresh graves of the two young men in the little cemetery there.

From the Mowry Mine, a short distance from today's town of Patagonia, the travelers journeyed to several other small mines known to be in the area, and at length crossed the Santa Rita Mountains to come once again to Tubac. Supplies were again low, so a detail was sent to Tucson for them while the rest of the party waited in camp. Re-supplied, the travelers turned southward once again toward Poston's old mine at the Cerro Colorado, or "Red Hill." They passed two formerly great ranches, the Revanton Ranch and the Sopori Ranch, both of which were deserted. At the mine there was again nothing but ruin and desolation. The mine shaft, 140 feet deep, was partially filled with water. The adobe houses were fast falling down, and the piles of rich ore which were abandoned had been plundered by the Mexicans. Such was the entire southern Arizona region during the Civil War, while the barbaric Apaches held full command unchecked by any military power in either the United States or Mexico.

Only seven miles southwest of Cerro Colorado they visited the ruins of the headquarters of the vast, storied Arivaca ranch, then struck toward the Mexican border again, crossing at Sasabe, a border point even today. The Poston party circled the south end of the Baboquivari Mountains, visited the mines at Fresnal, and returned to Tucson. All of this journey was without incident. From Tucson the party returned to the Pima Villages, where Browne took leave of his host, Charles Poston, and his other companions.

His return trip was described in only a few sentences by Browne. "Mr. J. B. Allen gave me a seat in his buggy as far as

Yuma," he wrote. "There I met an old friend, Mr. Ames, superintendent of the Military Express, who had just arrived from Camp Drum ... We crossed the Colorado Desert and reached Los Angeles without serious incident, and in a few days more I was safely landed in San Francisco." In those few words he retraced a journey that he had described, on the way in, by using up half of an entire book. He wrote a series of articles based on this journey through Arizona, which were collected and published in a book in 1869. Its title was "Adventures in the Apache Country: A Tour through Arizona and Sonora, 1864."

The routes traveled by Browne, Poston and their companions are still there to be traveled by us today. Most are modern freeways and highways; in the southern mountains if not paved they are graded and graveled. Death on the road now has a different meaning from a sudden fusillade of arrows and bullets from a roadside thicket. And our appreciation of a visit to places such as Casa Grande, San Xavier, Tubac, Tumacacori or Arivaca may be sharpened by seeing them as they once were through the eyes of J. Ross Browne.

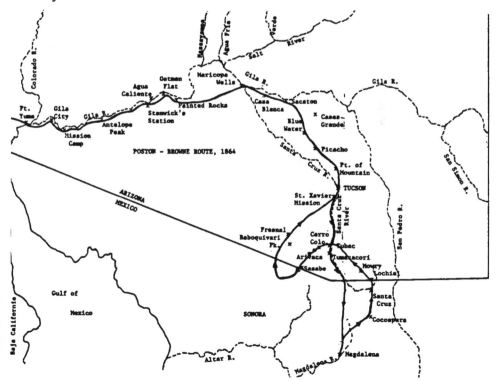

CHAPTER 5
Arizona's Classic Gun Duel

Arizona Territory in the 1870's and 1880's saw many gun battles, the most celebrated being, of course, the "gunfight at the O. K. Corral" in Tombstone when Wyatt Earp and his brothers, Virgil and Morgan, with Doc Holliday, shot it out with Billy Clanton and Tom and Frank McLowery.

High on the list is the shoot-out in Holbrook in which Sheriff Commodore Perry Owens slew four outlaws and their relatives while escaping unscathed himself, the fight at the Tewksbury ranch house in Pleasant Valley between them and their partisans on one side against the Grahams and theirs on the other, and the battle at the Stockton ranch east of Tombstone by Deputy Billy Breakenridge's posse attempting to arrest outlaws Zwing Hunt and Billy Grounds, in which all were killed or wounded except Breakenridge, who alone escaped without a scratch.

It saw also numerous gun duels in which it was just one man against another, at the end of which one lay lifeless in the dust, and the other if still alive himself faced one of several consequences. That might include trial and acquittal, or conviction meaning a stretch in Yuma Penitentiary or hanging, or lynching by a vigilante mob. Such were duels in Tombstone when Luke Short polished off Charlie Storms, Roger King's gunning down Johnnie Wilson, and Shotgun Collins' killing of Red Mike Shirley in a handkerchief duel. In Prescott, stage agent Joe Evans killed driver Johnnie Carroll in a duel in which Evans also lost his right arm as a result. The most famous of these gun duels, for fifty years thereafter the topic of conversation between Arizonans of that day, was that involving Joe Phy and Pete Gabriel in Florence.

The reason it was not soon forgotton was that Phy and Gabriel were both law officers who had held posts ranging from jailor to constable to deputy to sheriff. They had held these posts in several other towns prior to Florence, and were widely known and respected throughout the territory. They had mutual friends all over Arizona, and had themselves been friends for a long time before the differences arose that made them mortal enemies. Their final gun duel in the Tunnel Saloon in Florence shocked people all over the territory, made newspaper headlines for days, and for the next half-century was the subject of conversation whenever men of their day gathered.

Phy was born Josephus Phy at Sedalia, Missouri, in 1845. The family moved to Texas as farmers, but the parents died, and Joe was left in his brother Isaac's care. This proved to be an oppressive relationship for young Joe. Somewhere along the line the Phys had become family friends with the Granville Ourys, who had moved to and become established in Tucson. Granville Oury and his brother, William, became two of the most famous pioneers of Arizona Territory, deeply respected, and the holders of many important political offices. Mrs. Granville Oury let Joe know that the boy would be welcome in Tucson, so at the age of fifteen he ran away from home to Tucson, taking his violin, his only pleasure.

Joe Phy, killed in a gun duel with Pete Gabriel in the Tunnel Saloon in Florence, 1888. There seems to be no picture of Gabriel. (Courtesy Arizona Historical Society)

When he was old enough, the Oury family set up young Joe in the freighting business, and he began freighting out of Wickenburg. His use of dray horses was the first to be seen in Arizona. Not only was his business successful, he proved to be absolutely fearless in the face of danger. Once when driving a six-mule team toward Prescott through Skull Valley with a load of supplies, he and a man with him named McNutty were stopped by a band of Indians. They told him just to turn his animals and load over to them, and they would spare the men's lives. Phy unhitched the lead mules, sent McNutty to Prescott on one of them for help, grabbed his rifle, and held off the Indians for three hours. McNutty returned with a posse at his back and the Indians, seeing the riders approaching, immediately fled.

Evidently Joe did not stay with his freighting venture very long, successful as it might have been. Possibly it just turned out to be too dull. The reminscences of one John Mahoney state that Mahoney "kept a stage station four miles south of Date Creek, where Tom Harris and Sam Columbo were murdered by two Mexicans. At first it was thought by Indians, but Joe Phy who was deputy then at Wickenburg was there after the murder and said no Indians ever done it. He left and in about ten days we got the news Joe tracked them to somewhere on the Gila and killed both of them. On them he found some of the property they took. Besides, one of them in the tussle with Sam got hold of Sam's knife and had a bad cut across the palm of his right hand . . ."

Not long thereafter was the incident recounted elsewhere in this book, that Joe was in Phoenix when a man was disturbing the peace by brandishing a shotgun. Sheriff Tom Barnum deputized Phy on the spot to stop that nonsense, and Joe commandeered a horse hitched at the sidewalk. A short time later he reported to Barnum that the man was lying dead by the roadside a half-mile out.

In 1874 William Oury, brother of Joe Phy's benefactor Granville Oury, was the sheriff of Pima County and Joe was the county jailor. Two men were brought in who had murdered two Mexican sheepherders at Blue Water station on the old Gila trail. Their names were William Hall and one Moore. Hall was tried for murder and sentenced to 99 years in Yuma prison, but on January 1, 1875, he, Moore and two other prisoners broke jail and fled toward the Old Mexico line. Joe Phy, now a deputy sheriff, in April got a tip on where Hall might be hiding in Mexico, and with another deputy set out to bring him back. They sneaked into Mexico, captured Hall, and made it back to American soil. But while Phy was sleeping, the prisoner slipped his shackles and fled back into Mexico. This time Phy hired another Mexican to go after Hall, who was again captured and brought back to Arizona. Joe delivered him to Sheriff Oury, who gave Phy the satisfaction of delivering the slippery murderer to Yuma.

Political fortunes being what they are, and the political "spoils system" being even more prevalent then than now, Joe was soon out at Tucson and back in Phoenix. In June, 1878, the *Arizona Enterprise* of Prescott stated that Joe Phy, who had served the county long and well "in a minor capacity" was the leading candidate for Maricopa County Sheriff, and if elected would make an energetic officer. On May 11, 1878, the *Salt River Herald* said that "yesterday Joe Phy took two pistols away from a man who was racing around our streets . . . having too much of our salt water that is retailed at a bit a glass in him." On July 20, 1878, the *Herald* reported that "Tuesday morning several Mexicans, having too much 'tanglefoot' on board, got into difficulty in one of their bagnios, and for a time it looked as if blood would be shed. Officer Phy put a stop to it, and probably that was the cause of the assault being made upon him in the afternoon."

In that assault, Phy had been sent to quell a disturbance in a residence, and was struck over the head with a blunt instrument and thrown into a ditch. One Jose La Cruz was bound over to the grand jury on a charge of assault to commit murder on Phy, and, said the *Herald* on July 27, 1878, "unable to give said bonds in the sum of $1,000 he is occupying quarters in the county jail growing fat on three meals a day." Joe was near death from this beating and recovered very slowly. But in September a stage robber escaped from the guard house at Fort Whipple near Prescott, stole a horse, and headed for the Mexican border. Alerted that the culprit was headed his way, Phy captured him and delivered him back to Prescott.

Despite being described as the leading candidate for Maricopa County Sheriff by newspapers in Phoenix and Prescott, Phy lost the election, and on January 1, 1879, the *Herald* stated that "Joe Phy, for a long time deputy sheriff of this county, has gone to Tucson to locate." There he went into the business of furnishing water in that community with a brother of Mrs. Granville Oury,

Dobbs' Halfway Station (Dobbs' Well) in 1884, was 49 miles west of Tucson on the road to Quijotoa mining camp, 97 miles from Tucson. Stage driver known only as Hank was killed a few weeks later by stage robbers. Others from left are Mrs. Dobbs holding son Tom, a mining man named Carlile, station-keeper E. W. Dobbs, and half-breed Indian wrangler. Note 'olla' on table behind Mrs. Dobbs, chickens on the ground behind horses. Identification by T. W. Dobbs. (Courtesy Arizona Historical Society)

Adam Sanders. They leased a spring on land owned by Granville Oury, ran a tank truck to homes, selling water at twenty-five cents per pail, had a bath house at the spring where baths went for twenty-five cents each, and owned a sprinkler wagon that watered down the city's dusty streets. Though successful, the business ended when the city's first water mains were installed. It was during this time that Joe Phy met Pete Gabriel, who had been elected sheriff of Pinal County, and who offered Joe a job as deputy if he would relocate in Florence. This Joe did when the water business ended.

A great deal of information about Pete Gabriel is found at the Arizona Historical Society in the reminiscences of Mike Rice, an Arizona pioneer newspaperman and law officer. Gabriel was born in Prussia around 1840 and came to California with his parents who died shortly thereafter. Young Pete was taken into the home of a Judge Whitesides in Yuba City. He showed what he was made of in his early teens when the judge's wife was about to give birth. The presence of a doctor was absolutely necessary, but the only one was on the other side of the Yuba River which was at a raging flood stage. No one could be found who would brave the river except Pete, who assured the judge that he would bring the doctor or die in the attempt. Saddling a horse, he mounted and plunged with the animal into the swift-flowing flood, gained the opposite bank, and coerced the doctor into going with him. At the river bank the doctor demurred, but Pete shoved the doctor's horse into the river, steered it by the tail and made it across again so that the doctor could attend the wife.

Once on his own, Gabriel made his way to Idaho where he first appeared as a deputy sheriff in a mining district where he got his baptism among the claim-jumpers and other ruffians. Returning to Los Angeles in 1872 or 1873, he became a deputy sheriff there under Sheriff Billy Rowlands. In the spring of 1874 a judge issued writs of eviction on several settlers who had squatted on the Workman ranch illegally. Several deputies served the writs on all the squatters except one Pat Newman who had pre-empted a claim, built a house, and gave every indication of intending to stay. He barricaded himself in the cottage and resisted service with the aid of a double-barreled shotgun, threatening instant death to anyone who approached his doorway.

Having served all of the writs except the one on Newman, the bluffed deputies returned to town, sheepish and crestfallen, and reported to the sheriff the failure of their mission. Sheriff Rowlands was himself an absolutely fearless man and would have had no qualms about serving the writ on Newman himself, but decided to try diplomacy first. He had another deputy whom he knew to be fearless and efficient — and a personal friend of Newman. That man was Pete Gabriel. He entrusted the writ to Pete with the admonition to use caution, but to serve it on Newman.

Gabriel saddled his horse, rode out to Newman's house, unlatched the gate and leisurely strolled toward the front door. Newman watched Gabriel's approach, got up on a table shoved against the inside of the door, poked his double-barreled shotgun through the transom over the door, and called on Gabriel to halt. He told Pete he knew why he was there and would not be served with the writ of eviction by him or anyone else. Pete answered, "Pat, we've been friends a long time, and I appreciate your position, but as an officer of the law I have to serve this writ and as a friend I advise you to accept service and save us both from disagreeable consequences."

Newman replied, "Pete, I don't want to hurt you, but if you attempt to break in this door you do so at your own risk." Gabriel continued to advance, Newman cried once more, "Halt, or I'll shoot!" and then fired the double charge into Gabriel's chest. The buckshot tore a hole in it large enough to hold a billiard ball and completely destroyed the left lung. Doctors gave little hope of Gabriel's recovery, but when the buckshot had been removed he showed signs of improvement. It was weeks before they could even give assurance of his recovery.

The trial of Newman was spectacular, as Gabriel was carried into court every day on a stretcher, and the best lawyers to be found argued the case. Newman, however, was found guilty of assault with intent to commit murder and sentenced to ten years in the penitentiary. Gabriel recovered, but the chest wound troubled him all the rest of his life. He resigned as deputy and took a job with the stage company whose route terminated at Ehrenberg in Arizona, on the Colorado River, and headquartered at Wickenburg. Newman's lawyer eventually got him a new trial, and Gabriel was summoned from Wickenburg as a witness. But Gabriel, being outside the jurisdiction of the California court, refused to return. He sent word that he would not appear against Newman again, that he believed the man had been punished enough by the time spent in prison, and that he himself would have acted as Newman did under similar circumstances. Newman was acquitted at the second trial, and Gabriel sent him a letter congratulating him on the result.

While at Wickenburg in 1876 as agent for the stage line, Gabriel was playing poker in a bar one day. He detected a crooked gambler in the game holding out cards, and called him on it. The gambler whipped out a knife, but before he could use it Pete had drawn his six-gun and shot the man through the heart. He was tried in Prescott for this shooting and acquitted.

Gabriel moved to Tucson, where he was appointed a deputy sheriff under the then sheriff of Pima County, Peter R. Brady, Sr. Brady was a famous pioneer Arizonan, who was in on various enterprises, including part ownership of the famed but ill-starred Vekol Mine, and ran for territorial delegate to Congress. It was while a deputy under Brady that Gabriel became acquainted with Joe Phy, plying his water business in Tucson. In time, Gabriel

The Tunnel Saloon in Florence about 1885, where in 1888 the gun duel between Joe Phy and Pete Gabriel took place. Note false front on adobe building. In the picture are, from left, a Mexican boy, W.H. Kearms, ex-soldier, John H. Holgate, farmer, Manuel S. Ramirez, clerk in charge of the Fish and Collingwood Store and well-known in Florence, Judge Frank Stillman, Justice of the Peace and jeweler, Capt. John G. Keating, owner of the saloon, and William Carpenter. (Courtesy Arizona Historical Society)

moved to Florence, seat of the newly-formed Pinal County, where he was appointed a deputy sheriff and was eventually elected the sheriff of Pinal County.

One of his first official acts was the execution of a Mexican murderer. The old adobe jail in Florence was not properly equipped for the event, so Pete had a gallows constructed out on the mesa near Adamsville, four miles west and long a ghost town. Hundreds of townspeople, Pima and Maricopa Indians gathered on the mesa on the appointed day. Gabriel, though he never shirked a duty, was reluctant to inflict the death penalty, so he appointed a special deputy named Tom Kerr to adjust the rope and spring the trap. When the prisoner ascended the scaffold, was strapped and had the noose placed around his neck, the condemned man pushed Kerr to one side, exclaiming, "I don't want you to touch me. I want my friend Don Pedro to do this job." So Gabriel, without further ado, seized the handle and sprang the trap.

As an aside to this affair, according to Mike Rice, this man Tom Kerr met a fate more tragic than the Mexican's in later years. Kerr had a record as a cold-blooded killer from Idaho to Arizona, one of his more dastardly acts being the shooting of a blind man in Globe. Kerr murdered a young man at Pioneer, a town in the Pinal Mountains near Globe, and was lynched by an infuriated mob. Before he was strung up, he begged that his shoes be removed and piteously appealed for time to write a letter to his sister. His requests were refused, the mob crying out "You did not give your victim time to write letters to his sisters." Suiting the actions to the words, a score or more of husky miners pulled on the rope, and left him adorning the limb of a pine tree with his shoes on.

Bad men avoided Pete Gabriel like the plague, and with ample reason, according to Mike Rice who also became a deputy under Gabriel. One such hombre continually, when Gabriel had occasion to be out of town, harassed the citizens of Florence by shooting up the saloons and compelling the unwilling bartenders to set up drinks for equally unwilling imbibers. One time he had been especially obnoxious when Pete, who had just returned to town, got wind of the shenanigans. Mike was in the office talking with undersheriff George Evans when Gabriel came in spitting fire. "What's this I hear?" he demanded of Evans, "and what in hell do I have an undersheriff for who permits such actions in my absence?"

Stung by this, Evans answered, "Pete, I don't care to come in contact with this man, as I might have to kill him in trying to arrest him. Besides, he has often said he's not afraid of you, and even you could not arrest him."

"He said that, did he?" Gabriel replied. "We'll see into that." Turning to Rice, he asked where the man could be found, and Rice told him "At Pisano's saloon." Gabriel told Rice to come along with him, and together they visited all the saloons on Main Street. They learned that the object of their search was at Pisano's Saloon in the rear of the post office.

Turning the corner, they came in sight of the man they sought in front of the saloon, his horse's head in the doorway. He was brandishing his gun, threatening the bar patrons. Seeing Gabriel approach, he whirled his horse around, spurred its flanks, and made a run for it. Gabriel called on him three times to halt, but the rider continued his mad race. Gabriel raised his six-gun and fired just one shot at a distance of 150 yards. Horse and rider went down in an irrigation ditch. When Gabriel and Rice reached the spot, the horse was dead as a mackerel and the rider lying partly beneath it. He was still alive, but in attempting to stand crumpled to the sidewalk and died before he reached the jail. The doctor found that the bullet had pierced the rider's back below the shoulder blade, passed through his chest, and struck the horse behind the ears, killing the beast instantly. Gabriel always maintained he had aimed only to cripple the horse, and thus arrest the rider.

On another occasion a Mexican wanted in Florence for some law violation was traced by Gabriel to Tucson. Arriving there, Gabriel found that the fugitive had been tipped off, and had fled. On his way out, he had kidnapped a young girl from the barrio, and headed for the Mexican border. Gabriel hitched up a team to a buckboard and followed the man's trail over the road to Quijotoa, coming in sight of him beyond Dobb's Well. The fleeing man recognized who his pursuer was and put whip and spurs to his horse, but was handicapped in his flight by the fact that the girl was riding in front of him on the saddle.

When Gabriel got close enough to take a shot, he had to be careful not to hit the girl. The road over which they were racing had numerous dips, where they would lose sight of each other. At an opportune time, when the Mexican appeared on a ridge in a curve of the road and broadside in view, Gabriel jumped from the buckboard, braced his Winchester on the seat and fired, bringing the man out of the saddle mortally wounded. Gabriel placed the terrified girl in the buckboard and returned her unharmed to her family, leaving the abductor to the coyotes.

Such were the two men who were one day to fight it out to the death between them. When Phy had settled up his water business in Tucson, he moved to Florence and went to work under Sheriff Pete Gabriel as jailor and deputy. This may have been part time or intermittent duty, as the Florence newspapers carried stories of other enterprises in which Phy engaged. On July 25, 1885, the *Arizona Weekly Enterprise* of Florence stated that "Sheriff

Gabriel and Joe Phy left for Tonto Basin Wednesday after horse thieves." On August 15, 1885, the *Enterprise* said, "Sheriff Gabriel and Mr. Joseph Phy returned Tuesday from their protracted chase after the fellow who has Goldburg's horses. Goldburg lives in New Mexico and sent the man in question over into Texas with $2,500 to buy cattle. Instead of buying cattle the fellow bought horses and brought them to Arizona to start a horse ranch of his own. Goldburg . . . got Sheriff Gabriel and Mr. Phy to go after the thief, stating the last trace he had of him was in Tonto Basin.

"When the officers arrived at Tonto they found that the culprit had moved on. They took up the trail and followed it into Apache County and found where the man was, but could not catch him. He was hid away in the hills and there were about fifteen or twenty men carrying provisions to him and keeping him informed as to the officers' movements. Under the circumstances it was impossible to capture him and the officers returned. They had a hard trip and lived upon short rations most of the time." The above story is revealing. Phy and Gabriel lived close together for an entire month, in danger and on short rations. One can readily imagine the friendship springing up between two strong, courageous and

Interior of the Tunnel Saloon in Florence, owner Capt. John Keating behind the bar. (Courtesy Arizona Historical Society)

determined men under such circumstances, and the confidences shared over the month's campfires. Of such are lasting friendships made.

On September 5th, 1885, the *Enterprise* reported that "Mr. Joseph Phy arrived from Tucson this week with his teams and three wagons. He has contracted to deliver 1,000 cords of wood at Pinal for the Silver King company, and has gone up there to commence work." This reference is to the rich Silver King mine near today's Superior, and to its nearby town of Pinal City located near the Southwest Arboretum of today. It must have taken six months to cut and deliver the wood, for on March 27, 1886, the *Enterprise* stated that "Mr. Joseph Phy has sent to Tucson for his water wagons and will go into the water business here. He will furnish the best water to be had and will be liberally patronized."

In that same March 27, 1886, issue, the *Enterprise* carried the following: "Jesus Para, the Mexican who robbed Mr. C. M. Marshal of Casa Grande, and was subsequently shot and brought to the jail here, has recovered from his wound and escaped Tuesday afternoon. The jailor, Mr. Joseph Phy, had him and another prisoner chopping down some of the cottonwood trees in front of the court house. He ordered Para to carry a load of wood into the house, but when the prisoner reached the corner of the building he darted around it, jumped over the adobe fence, and ran for the brush west of Colonel Ruggles' house." Phy tried to pursue him, but it was useless, so Joe ran back to get a horse. He found Sheriff Gabriel just mounting up, and Pete took up the trail. There is no word whether the escapee was caught, but the article confirms that Phy was still in the sheriff's department at that time.

Phy always claimed that Gabriel had promised to see that Phy became sheriff when Gabriel retired from the office. The friendship between the two men was cooling because of some minor incidents, but whether with Gabriel's assistance or not Phy was nominated by acclamation for sheriff of Pinal County at the Democratic convention in September, 1886. One incident told of them is that Phy owned a suitcase, something new in those days, of which he was inordinately proud. Gabriel was called suddenly to California and borrowed Phy's suitcase for the trip without Joe's knowledge. Upon his return, Phy castigated Gabriel for his presumption, leading to words between the two men. As such things will happen, one word led to another until the friendship was beyond repair.

Though there were two other candidates in the sheriff's contest, Jere Fryer and M. W. Harter, Phy was heartily endorsed in the newspapers and was apparently the favorite to win. An incident in October, a month before the election, ended his chances and escalated his animosity against his former friend, Pete Gabriel, to a white-hot hatred. Thomas Montgomery was a faro dealer from Globe, well-known and respected, as gambling was then a profession with little or no stigma attached. He told Gabriel and others that Phy had made the remark that he had been sent out to beat a scrub for sheriff, demeaning to his opponents. Hearing Montgomery make this statement in a crowd, Gabriel drew him to one side and told him he should be careful about making a statement of that kind, as it would certainly be injurious to Phy's chances. Montgomery claimed that it was true, and he had witnesses to prove it.

This alleged remark by Phy became blown all out of proportion to its importance. When one day Montgomery passed through Florence on his way to Casa Grande, Gabriel told Montgomery that he would be called upon to prove his statement. Montgomery replied that he was ready to produce witnesses present when Phy made the remark. Then Phy was told of the rumored slight, and emphatically denied that he had said it. He said he was ready to deny it to his accuser's face. Apprehensive over the escalation of feelings over this usually minor matter, and expecting to be called away for a period of time, Gabriel suggested that he and some friends go with Phy to Casa Grande, confront Montgomery, and get the matter straightened out. Thus, late in September, 1886, Gabriel, Phy, and two friends traveled to Casa Grande.

The party arrived at about nine at night, had supper, then began looking for Montgomery. They headed for a saloon to get some cigars, asking Phy to come along. Phy replied that he did not smoke, or drink, but that he would walk along with them. They went in, not noticing that Montgomery was there, sitting among the crowd. Phy, however, soon spotted him, approached and asked, "Is this Tom Montgomery?" The latter answered affirmatively, to which Phy replied, "You have lied about me, and will have to take it back or fight." Montgomery jumped up, and Phy struck him with his fist and knocked him to his knees. Montgomery, a large and powerful man, seized a chair, whereupon

Phy struck him over the head with a pistol. The friends then intervened and dragged Phy away to his room.

After they had talked to him, Phy cooled off and said he was ready to submit to arrest. It didn't take long: Gabriel as sheriff had a warrant and promptly served it on Phy who waived the preliminary hearing and was released on bond. Gabriel also cancelled Phy's appointment as deputy sheriff and took his gun and knife away from him. This so enraged Phy that he offered to fight it out right then and there with Gabriel "as men fight," but Gabriel only laughed and said, "Joe, this is only part of my job." From that time on Phy's hatred for Gabriel became an obsession — a mania — with him.

The Florence *Enterprise*, in reporting the confrontation, tried to play down its importance and sought to excuse Phy. "Coming unexpectedly upon Montgomery," said the newspaper, "and feeling keenly the unprovoked and gross injustice he had suffered at the hands of Montgomery, it was perfectly natural that Mr. Phy should have called him to account at once. Any man who is frank, honest, impulsive and courageous, like Mr. Phy, would have done the same thing under the same circumstances." Other newspapers in the territory, particularly those of Phoenix and Prescott, editorialized along the same lines and continued to support Phy as the best man for the job of sheriff. But, after the election early in November, the *Enterprise* reported the vote count in its November 20, 1886, issue. Fryer was elected with 346 votes, Harter had 249 votes, and Phy ran last with 209 votes.

After his arrest by Gabriel, Phy never lost an opportunity to abuse him to his face or behind his back, to defame or abase him in any way possible, often within Gabriel's hearing. Knowing that Phy was trying to goad him into a confrontation, Gabriel never replied in kind, avoiding him whenever possible. Phy was ambidextrous and a crack shot with either hand. He practiced his six-gun skills for hours at a time. Despite Gabriel's efforts to avoid it, all of Florence knew that it was only a matter of time before the show-down came. The time was a year and a half.

Phy was boarding with Peter Brady, Jr., in Florence. The evening of one day he had been especially moody, Phy suddenly took his shotgun from a corner, slipped buckshot shells into it, and started for the door. When Brady inquired where he was going, Phy replied, "I am going to kill that damned Pete Gabriel."

Brady told him that, if he did that, he need never return to his home. This caused Phy to think twice about what he was about to do, he regained his composure, and returned the shotgun to its place.

Gabriel himself had his unreasonable moments. His wife was much younger than he, and though she bore him three children, Pete could become insanely jealous. For this reason, they were living apart. Gabriel would become furious if ever he noticed his wife talking to Phy at any social function. One day Gabriel and Rice were talking in Fryer's office when through the window they noticed Phy standing in the street some 200 feet away. Presently, Gabriel's little daughter approached Phy and handed him a note, which Joe started to read. Gabriel seized a rifle, jumped to his feet, and raised it to fire. Rice grabbed Gabriel's arm and pulled as Phy stepped around the corner, avoiding instant death. Rice persuaded Gabriel to put down the rifle and not follow Phy. The note turned out to be an order for groceries, which Phy had been asked to pick up and deliver to the house.

It was on Thursday, May 31, 1888, that the climactic gun duel between Joe Phy and Pete Gabriel that everyone had been expecting for so long took place. Phy had spent two weeks in Tucson visiting friends and had just returned to Florence. Gabriel had been at a gold mining claim he owned in the Dripping Springs Mountains east of Florence, and had returned to Florence to obtain supplies, pay bills and see his friends. He and Mike Rice had driven in from Riverside Station, arriving about an hour before sundown. They had been well-stocked with booze on the trip and Pete, according to Rice, was more than "three sheets to the wind" when they arrived at the old Pinto House where they had been batching. Instead of going to his room, however, Gabriel wandered downtown for some social life.

Though having had more than a little booze, Gabriel was armed and wary. In John Keating's Tunnel Saloon, he glanced out the back window and saw Phy watching him. Knowing then that Phy was stalking him, Gabriel decided to stay in the saloon, thinking that if he went outside Phy would take a potshot at him. He was standing at the bar, drinking with Pete Brady, and people who came in said that whenever anyone came through the door, Gabriel would reach for his six-gun, tucked in his waistband. Witnesses saw Phy approach the swinging front doors of the Tunnel Saloon, and pause for a moment before entering. They differed on whether he had a gun in his hand, but most said he had a gun in one hand and a knife in the other. In the saloon besides Gabriel were Brady, Keating, and three or four others who hit the floor or fled out the back door when Phy entered the front.

As the swinging doors burst open, Gabriel turned toward the door, and said "Joe!" with his hand flashing toward his gun. Phy fired, striking Gabriel in the chest just below the heart, the bullet hitting his one good lung. Gabriel, despite the shock of the bullet, fired back, striking Phy in the pit of the stomach. Eleven shots were fired, one of the first putting out the lights. In the semi-darkness Gabriel staggered forward, shooting as he went, hitting Phy again in the thigh breaking both bones, in the shoulder and wrist. Another shot from Phy struck Gabriel in the right groin, coming out close to his spine and kidneys. Phy staggered out through the front door and fell on the sidewalk with his legs in the gutter. Gabriel followed him out, staggering as he went, and slowly collapsed between the door and the sidewalk.

People came running toward the scene from all directions, knowing that what they had been expecting for so long had finally

The last location of the famed Tunnel Saloon was where this building now stands, 350 Main Street, Florence. The vacant lot, left, was the saloon's location where the Phy-Gabriel fight took place. The original buildings were destroyed by fire in 1924.

taken place. Phy had raised himself on one elbow. Dave Gibson approached him and asked, "Joe, are you hurt much?" to which Phy replied, "Go away from me, you murdering _____," at the same time slashing at the man with his knife, cutting his leg to the bone just above the knee. Others carried Phy to the stage office, to where the town doctor, a Dr. William Harvey, was summoned to attend to his wounds. Little could be done, and Phy's condition worsened. Phy's last words were to ask whether Gabriel would live. He was told by the doctor, who could not have known since he had not attended Gabriel, that Gabriel's hours were numbered. Believing that he had killed his mortal enemy, Joe Phy died at about half an hour past midnight.

According to Mike Rice, he reached Gabriel's side before Pete collapsed on the sidewalk. Mike asked if Pete was hurt. Gabriel replied, "Yes, he got me, but I always told you that if he shot me through the heart I would still get him, and I did." Gabriel was carried to a one-room adobe house next to the sheriff's office and placed on a cot. His friends, men and women, crowded in and someone asked if Dr. Harvey had been notified. The reply was that Harvey was attending Joe Phy but would arrive soon. Hearing this, Gabriel exclaimed, "What! My family physician attending my enemy before coming here? Tell him I won't have his services. I don't want him here."

As there was no doctor nearer than the Pima Indian agency at Sacaton, a courier was immediately dispatched to Dr. Sabin, the agency's physician and surgeon. Sabin arrived about four the next morning, and upon examining Gabriel, pronounced him fatally wounded. He said, "Pete, if you have any business to settle, do so at once, as you cannot live another twenty-four hours. You have been shot through the intestines and the right lung, and your case is hopeless." To this Gabriel replied, "Doctor, you say I am shot through the lungs? Well, I had one lung shot away in Los Angeles years ago, but by God, I will beat you to it and be without lungs a better man than any of my enemies." According to Mike Rice, Gabriel was up and around in thirty days, though his wounds never completely healed and thus he never fully recovered.

Following the Phy-Gabriel gun duel, the *Enterprise* printed a full account in its June 2, 1888, edition. "The whole affair," said the newspaper, "is one to be regretted by all people, and the sad consequences are far too serious a sequel to the inadequate causes that led up to the tragedy." In its next weekly edition, on June 9th, the *Enterprise* printed the entire testimony of all the witnesses at the coroner's inquest, and the verdict: "We, the undersigned coroner's jury, in the case of J. Phy, find he came to his death by a gunshot wound by J. P. Gabriel, and it was done in self defense." It was signed by the nine members of the coroner's jury. There is no report that Gabriel was ever summoned to a hearing over the shooting.

"I personally know," wrote Mike Rice many years later, "that Phy's death haunted and harrassed (Gabriel) during the remainder of his life. Some four years after Phy's death, Pete and I were out on a trip . . . We went into camp at Desert Well and . . . shared the same blankets. On this night, about midnight it was, Gabriel in a state of somnambulism drew his six-shooter and crying "Joe, Joe, Joe" with each shot, emptied his pistol in the air, and fell back on the blankets in a state of complete collapse. As usual, he had hit the bottle continuously the preceding day. This incident frightened me badly. When he was sound asleep again, I reached over and took the revolver to my side of the bed . . . I then determined that I would never travel with Gabriel alone if he carried liquor . . ."

Gabriel lived another ten years, then died at his mining camp in the peace and quiet of the Dripping Springs Mountains, far from the turbulent scenes of his career as a law officer. The Florence *Tribune* on August 6, 1898, reported: "Ex-sheriff P. J. Gabriel died last Saturday morning at three a.m. (July 29th) at his camp at the Monitor Mine on Mineral Creek. He had been sick at his cabin for more than a week, alone and unattended, when his partner, Mr. McAllister, came to see him and found him lying very low. Every attention possible was given him, but without avail. The cause of death is not known, but it is supposed the water he had been drinking was strongly impregnated with arsenical and other mineral poisons (from the mining process.) . . . The body was buried at the mine."

Down through the years this desperate affray came to be known as Arizona's classic gun duel, and with the passage of time took on legendary proportions. Many were the stories told over campfires, in saloons and over supper, until the details were distorted and lurid. They were repeated by men who claimed to have witnessed it from start to finish, who had witnessed nothing. Accounts as authentic as could be other than the coroner's jury report carried in the newspaper were later written by Mike Rice, Arizona pioneer J. A. Rockfellow, and state historian Con P. Cronin. As late as 1935 the president of the Arizona Pioneers Association, Charles M. Clark, had the coroner's report as printed in the Florence *Enterprise* on June 9, 1888, re-printed in the *Arizona Republic* because he had so many inquiries about it.

So, when you visit old Florence, a unique Arizona history town, pause in front of 350 Main Street, once a location of the old Tunnel Saloon. Its location at the time of the Phy-Gabriel shoot-out was the vacant lot just south of 350 Main Street. Both buildings, of frame and adobe, were destroyed in a fire in 1924. Behind the present brick building is a roofed excavation, said to be the old "tunnel" from which the saloon took its name, a dugout with a canopy roof used as an annex to the saloon as a meeting room, and for drinking and card-playing. People are barred from going down into it, but no matter. Just driving by in your car the mind can take you back to that evening of May, 1888, and you might imagine hearing shots, and seeing two men stagger and fall after their deadly duel.

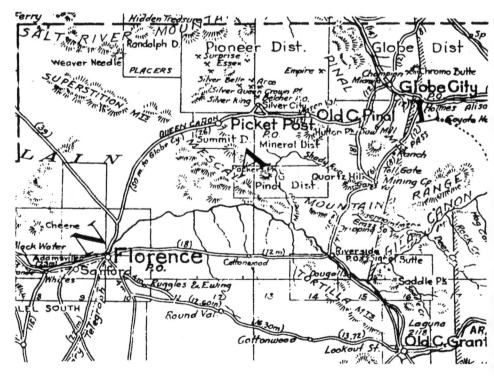

CHAPTER 6

Florence Was No Lady

If you have never journeyed to old Florence, the county seat of Pinal County, Arizona, you have been missing something. Your education in the history of Arizona's Old West will be incomplete until you have spent a day or two there. As a western heritage town, it rivals its more famous counterpart, Tombstone, as most of the buildings where historically famous incidents occurred are still intact, or partially so.

While Florence is proud of its heritage and certainly welcomes and tries to attract visitors, for some reason it seems not to want to play up its past as a raucous frontier town, which it undeniably was. The reminiscences of Mike Rice in the Arizona Historical Society in Tucson tattle on Florence. Rice was an Arizona pioneer well-known in his day, basically a newspaperman who sometimes worked in minor law enforcement offices. He lived for some time in Florence.

In the autumn of 1886 Jere Fryer was elected sheriff of Pinal County, defeating M. W. Harter and Joe Phy. Fryer was a resident of Casa Grande, and was handsome and personable as well as courageous and able. It hadn't hurt his election campaign at all that he was married to a beautiful and famous woman. Her name was Pauline Cushman. Born in New Orleans in 1833, she had grown up in Mississippi and was a highly successful actress when the Civil War broke out. Mike Rice described her as a woman of magnificent physique, with large, lustrous sloe-black eyes, black hair falling to her waist in ringlets, a lovely profile and a melodious voice. She became a Union spy, and though very successful with all those female attributes going for her, eventually she was caught and sentenced by the Confederacy to be hanged. The Union forces, however, captured the town where she was held and rescued her.

After the war, she made national personal appearance tours, and organized a troupe which went on a tour of western towns. She managed several California hotels as well as acting, then met and married Fryer who was fifteen years her junior. They moved to Casa Grande, then a boom town at the terminal of the railroad building across southern Arizona, and bought a hotel and livery stable. At Fryer's election as sheriff, Pauline was 53 years old, but still beautiful, was a good horsewoman and adept with guns. They bought a house in Florence, location of the sheriff's office.

From this absorbing distraction, necessary because she will figure in our story, we must return to our narrative. Fryer appointed Hinson Thomas his undersheriff, with several deputies, and Mike Rice as jailor. Thomas later was for years the U. S. Commissioner and a judge in Globe. Fryer and his appointees took office on January 1, 1887, and for some months there was comparative quiet. But, in August there arose a dispute between two farmers over water rights on the Gila River, some twelve miles upstream from Florence. The row was between James Brash and a man named White, who was of some prominence as the brother-in-law of District Judge Charles Silent.

Brash conspired with some young men to get rid of White, whom he accused of cutting him out of his water. The youths bushwhacked White and shot him to death. Promptly arrested along with Brash, they turned out to be two neighbor boys, Bud Dozier and Bob Dunn, and a transient named Emerson. When the latter managed to escape, Undersheriff Thomas got on his trail and arrested him at Willcox just as he was about to swing aboard a freight train. Thomas had a blacksmith shackle the prisoner and

Old Pinal County Court House in Florence as first built. Sheriff's office was at the two downstairs doors at the extreme left; above it the two jury room windows. Porticos added in 1904 obscured these windows. (Courtesy Pinal County Historical Society)

returned with him to Florence. En route, Thomas obtained a confession from Emerson, who turned state's evidence upon a promise of immunity from the county attorney. That made it necessary to keep Emerson apart from the other prisoners, who would have loved to get their hands on him.

One bright, moonlight night in August, Rice and the newly-elected county attorney, Richard Sloan, were sleeping on cots in front of the sheriff's office, as was their custom during the summer months. Anyone who has endured August nights without air conditioning will understand. The sheriff and undersheriff were out of town for several days, two other deputies were also absent, and Mike Rice was the sole custodian of the court house and jail. About eleven o'clock Mike was wakened by a hand gently touching his forehead. On looking up he saw one of the town characters, Jeff Bramlet, one of those harmless ne'er-do-wells who made a poor living by doing chores around saloons. Irritated at being wakened at that hour, Mike asked what the blankety-blank he meant by waking him up.

Bramlet whispered that he came with a 'tip' that the vigilantes were holding a meeting in the "tunnel," that they knew the sheriff was out of town, and they were coming to take Brash, Dozier, Dunn and Emerson out and lynch them. To Sloan, Mike exclaimed, "You heard that, Dick! What am I going to do?" to which Sloan replied, "I don't know what to tell you. You're in charge of the jail and it's up to you to take whatever action you think is proper." Rice decided to investigate first if possible, doubting the reliability of the information. Slipping on his trousers and shoes, he started for the "tunnel" to learn what he could of any vigilante action.

The "tunnel" was a large excavation in the center of a livery corral, about thirty by forty feet square and ten feet deep, with a canopy roof. It was an annex to the Tunnel Saloon fronting on Main Street, and was used for meetings, as there was no public hall in Florence. Capt. Jack Keating and Billy (Shotgun) Miller, an ex-Wells-Fargo shotgun guard, were the proprietors of the saloon and tunnel. Rice went down an alley to the corral, climbed over a six-foot adobe wall, and crept cautiously to the canopy over the tunnel entrance. He crawled up on the canopy and lay on his stomach, from which position he saw nothing but could hear distinctly.

Several of those present spoke for and against the lynching. It was finally decided that, Fryer and Thomas both being out of town, the party would storm the jail, overpower Rice and get his keys, take the prisoners from their cells, and lynch them. Having learned enough, Rice retreated down the alley to the jail. He called on Dave Gibson, who turns up in several other violent episodes in Arizona history, and persuaded him to help hold the prisoners. He went to Sheriff Fryer's home and woke his wife, described the situation to her, and said he intended to hold the prisoners at any cost.

Fryer's wife, Pauline, promised to hurry to the jail as soon as she could dress. Mike Rice ran back to the court house where he met Gibson at the sheriff's office. He stationed Gibson in a vacant room across the street from the jail with a sawed-off shotgun loaded with buckshot. When Mrs. Fryer arrived and asked for a six-shooter, he also suggested that she take a rifle, as Rice knew she was a good shot with it. She took her position in her husband's chair in his office. Sloan refused to get involved, so there were still only three against the mob.

Then the idea occurred to Rice to arm the prisoners and let them help in their own defense. The dangers also occurred to him; he would have to arm them, place them on their honor to return the guns if the danger passed, and take what might come. He woke the prisoners, Brash, Dozier, Dunn and Emerson, called them to the cell gates, and laid it on the line, thus: "You fellows know what it means when I tell you the vigilantes are in session in the tunnel, and are coming here to take you fellows out and strangle you. I am determined this will not happen while I am in charge. What I propose to do is to arm you men, take you upstairs into the grand jury room, and await whatever is to come. What I ask of you is to act as directed — make no move until I give the order.

"When the mob appears, I shall tell them I have four deputies fully armed, and that we will kill the first man who attempts an attack on the jail. What I want from you is your promise to do this, and to return your arms to me after we have beaten them off. It is squarely up to you. If you play square with me, well and good, but if you attempt to take advantage of me after this fight is over, I have two deputies properly placed who will shoot you down the minute they get the signal."

All promised to be fair, and Rice gave each of them a Winchester rifle with full magazines plus a handful of extra cartridges. He took a sawed-off shotgun for himself, and all went upstairs to the jury room over the sheriff's office.

The sashes had been removed from the two windows for summer ventilation, and Rice placed the prisoners so that they could shoot through the window openings if it became necessary. He called down to Mrs. Fryer that they were all ready for the mob. She called back, "So are we. You do your part and Dave and I will do ours." Almost instantly thereafter a mob of forty to fifty men rounded the corner, marching diagonally across the street toward the sheriff's office. Before they got too close, Rice stepped to the window, shotgun in hand in full view, and called to them to halt.

One of the leaders, whom Rice recognized as one Stuttering Jack McCoy, said, while stuttering, "You can't stop citizens on the streets of Florence at night!" Rice replied, loud enough for the entire gang to hear, "You dirty strangling skunks! If you come one step nearer the jail, I will fill you so full of lead that you will sink in a wash tub! Now listen — I have beaten you to it. I have four deputies with me to protect the jail and its contents, so you advance even a yard at your own peril." Turning to the prisoners, Rice said, "Come on, boys, show yourselves." They marched to the windows, rifles in hand and five guns were pointing downward. They had the desired effect. The mob scattered like a flock of quail escaping a load of bird shot.

Still, Mike Rice was far from home free. Here he was alone with four men, armed sufficiently to stand off a mob howling for their lives, men with the open doors of the penitentiary staring at them, and nothing between them and freedom except their vague promise to play the game fairly. From the time the lynch mob had dispersed until daybreak, Mike and his armed prisoners stood guard at the windows of the jury room, the longest hours of Mike's life. He did not fear anything from Brash, Dozier and Dunn, but he dreaded the final showdown with Emerson.

When daylight arrived, Rice asked the armed men what they were going to do, play marbles or quit the game. Brash flunked the test. He said, "Mike, what assurance do we have that if we give up the guns, and you lock us up, that the lynchers won't return and get us anyhow?" to which Rice replied, "The same assurances I gave you when I took you out of your cells. I want you boys to give me the rifles and return quietly to your cells." Dozier and

The old Pinal County Court House in Florence, now McFarland State Historic Park. In it Mike Rice and armed prisoners stood off a lynch mob in 1886, but in 1883 Joe Tuttle and Len Redfield were lynched, hanged from the rafters in the jail corridor (see Riverside chapter).

Dunn thereupon laid down their rifles, but Brash refused to surrender his. At this Emerson, the "bad man" Rice feared, quickly grasped Brash by the collar, shook him as a cat would a rat, made him lay down the rifle, and pointing to the corridor of the jail, marched Brash ahead of him down the stairway, still retaining his own rifle. Mike Rice, filled with apprehension, followed.

Descending the stairway, shotgun in hand, Mike still felt that his elevated position behind the men might give him a little edge if Emerson raised his gun to shoot him. He intended to let Emerson have the best that was in him before he could get into action. When the prisoners got to their cells, Emerson motioned them to enter, and following pulled the steel gate half ajar saying, "Come and get the gun, you are a fair man and I am just a man of my word." He handed Mike the rifle through the half-open steel door, pulled it closed, sprang the lever and incarcerated himself in his own cell.

Rice's action in arming the prisoners, however, made him 'persona non grata' in Florence. When Sheriff Fryer's bondsmen learned what had transpired, they threatened to withdraw their bond unless Fryer fired Rice. Fryer would not do that, but he did ask Rice to resign. Rice replied, "I'll see you in hell first. You hired me and you have a right to fire me, but I'll never admit by a forced resignation that I was in the wrong. On your own admission you approve of my act in arming the prisoners; besides, you have your prisoners safe in custody rather than at the end of a rope." Pat Holland, chairman of the Pinal County Board of Supervisors, came into the sheriff's office while Fryer and Rice were squabbling. He said to Fryer, "If your bondsmen want to quit, let them. I will have a bond for you by tomorrow." Next day, a wire came from Tucson stating that a $50,000 bond was ready for Fryer's signature.

This old courthouse and jail building still exists in Florence, on the National Register of Historic Places, owned by the State of Arizona. It was purchased by the late Sen. Ernest J. McFarland and donated to the state. Now it is known as McFarland Historic State Park, and most of the senator's papers are housed there. It is open to the public to view where this and other events historically famous took place. The appearance of the building has changed from the time Mike Rice and his prisoners held off the mob. In 1904 verandas were added around the east and south sides of the buildings, and they obscure the upstairs windows of the grand jury room over the old sheriff's office, through which Mike shouted into the street.

Not all of the reminiscences of Florence's early days are as filled with the electric aura of danger as the preceding. One of the recollections of Charles M. Clark, a well-known and respected Arizona pioneer, is of the following incident in Florence. In the summer of 1876 three Mexicans from the state of Chihuahua in Old Mexico rode into town on horseback, leading two pack horses. They put their animals in one of the corrals and instructed the corral boss to feed them plenty of hay and grain, as they had a hard trip ahead of them. The Mexicans spent several days around the Florence saloons, drinking and gambling, apparently well supplied with money. After about a week of getting acquainted, they allowed as how they thought one of their horses could out-run any three horses in the Florence country.

A Tartar Chinese named Jim Sam had a big gray horse that was fast for about a quarter of a mile. Jim Sam was a restaurant man, who at one time or another ran a restaurant in every town of any size in Arizona territory. He was a money-maker and a sport, and his particular hobby was horse-racing. Whenever Jim Sam entered his horse in a race, his restaurant, his cattle and his shirt were behind his horse. Lou Bailey, a Florence saloon-keeper, had a black gelding that also was fast and had a great get-away. Ex-sheriff Pete Gabriel had a favorite sorrel, a big rangy brute, that was a good, all-day horse.

The three Mexicans offered to run their horse a distance of nine miles against any three horses in the area, one man to ride the three horses changing his saddle to a new horse every three miles. Considerable interest was whipped up over the race, and the horses of Jim Sam, Lou Bailey and Pete Gabriel were selected to run against any horse the Mexicans might put up. It was contended that no horse could run nine miles against three fresh horses in relays, and win.

The Mexicans paraded their stock around the streets of Florence, that everybody might see them and form their own conclusions. Then the betting started. The Mexicans were well supplied with money, and for a day or two they were giving odds of 10 to 7, 10 to 6, and in some cases 10 to 5, with the Mexican horse on the short end. They took all bets, and before the Sunday on which the race was to be run they were betting even money on their horse. Selecting one of their pack horses which they called "Pajaro" (meaning "bird,") they started work on getting him into condition, and, said Charley Clark, "they knew their business. They cleaned the cockle-burrs out of his mane and tail, worked the loose hair off his hide, and exercised him every day. On race day his hide was so loose you could grab up a handful of it without distressing the horse in the least."

When the day of the race arrived, the Mexicans covered all the loose cash in the Gila valley. They had taken a bet from Jim Sam of $200 against his big gray horse, Bailey had pulled the bankrolls from all of his gambling games and bet it on the outcome, and Gabriel had secured all the loose cash his friends had and bet it against Pajaro. Everybody in the valley who had any money, horses or cattle had bet their last available cash or collateral against Pajaro, and at the last minute a couple of ranchers from just below Adamsville, a town four miles west of Florence, arrived driving thirty head of cattle to wager against the Mexican horse. The people of the entire valley were so eager to obtain a part of the Mexican's money that there was no cash in sight for heat bets — all bets were up on the final result.

The race started with Jim Sam's big gray as the first contender against Pajaro, for the first three miles. The heat was close with Pajaro leading by a head at the finish of the three miles. The relay rider then had to change his saddle to Bailey's black gelding before beginning the second lap. This delay allowed Pajaro to gain considerable distance, and this lap was the deciding lap of the race as Pajaro finished the six miles with a half-mile lead over the Bailey horse. When the rider had changed his saddle to Pete Gabriel's sorrel, Pajaro was out of sight. He finished the nine miles about half a mile to the good — winning all bets and breaking about every man in Florence.

The bets were all settled in about an hour after the finish. The three Mexicans started at once on their return trip to Chihuahua, driving about 300 head of cattle and about 30 to 40 head of horses, including Jim Sam's big gray. They also had won every dollar in cash available in the Florence district. "After the race," commented Charley Clark, "you could listen to an alibi from every one of the 100 or so men who were taken to a royal cleaning by the three Mexicans and their Pajaro horse."

The reminiscenses of Mike Rice, preserved in the Arizona Historical Society in Tucson, also reveal one of Florence's deep, dark secrets which is resurrected here and admittedly with some trepidation. According to Rice, sometime along in mid-summer of 1887, a couple of itinerant Italians came to Florence with a small circus outfit. The entourage consisted of a few trick ponies, a trained bear, and a large monkey, also well-trained and of almost human intelligence.

This outfit had left Tucson owing debts to merchants that they had failed to pay after purchasing supplies. A deputy constable had followed the deadbeats to Florence with a writ of attachment and levied it on the circus paraphernalia. They sold some of it and some of the animals, including the monkey, at auction. Living in Florence at that time, and for years thereafter, was a Mexican woman named Mrs. Corrales, but whose nickname was "Gusano" (meaning "worms.") She was famous for her abilities as a cook, particularly tamale and enchilada suppers. She had a large family of grandchildren whom she supported by her cooking, who, when the monkey was put up for sale, persuaded her to buy it for them as a playmate and pet.

The monkey soon became a popular addition to the Florence scene, and had entree not only to all the private homes, but to the lodge rooms and saloons as well — particularly the saloons. As it was a male, it followed certain habits of human males. It would enter a saloon, jump up on the counter, and by gibberish and motions demand a bottle and glass. Bartender Charley Starr, for whom the monkey formed a particular attachment, would put a few sugar cubes in a glass, pour into it a good stiff shot of booze, and give it to the monkey. The monk would then put his digits in the glass, dissolve the sugar, lap up the liquor to the last drop, and stagger out of the bar as tipsy as a drunken sailor.

One of its more ludicrous episodes occurred at an initiation ceremony in the Good Templar's Lodge. There was a harmless and likeable old character in the community named Minor, whose chief failing was overindulgence in the saloons, too. The fine ladies of the Good Templar's Lodge conceived the idea of reforming Minor by making him a member. Mike Rice notes that he had himself undergone such a reformation a year or so previously, and was at the time the Chief Templar of the Florence lodge. On the night of Minor's initiation, the lodge room was crowded to capacity. Minor stood before the altar, and Rice in deep solemnity was obligating the new member. Some of the street gang sneaked the monkey up the stairs and into the lodge room. Suddenly the monkey leaped up on the altar between Minor and Rice, demanding to take part in the ceremony. That was too much for Minor. With a yell of fright, he bolted down

Under this rubble-strewn cover at the rear of 350 Main Street is Florence's famous "tunnel," annex to the Tunnel Saloon, where in 1886 the mob planned the lynching of prisoners held in the county jail.

the steps four at a time, and never stopped until he reached his old stamping grounds at Picket Post near Superior. He was never seen in Florence again.

The monkey was teased and manhandled so much by mischievous boys and saloon rounders that eventually, in self-protection, it became combative and then aggressively vicious, resulting in numerous complaints to the sheriff's office and demands that it be confined or put to death. Everything came to a climax one day when a Mexican woman came to the sheriff's office, sobbing as if her heart would break. When Sheriff Jere Fryer questioned her about the cause of her sorrow, she replied, "The monkey has killed my baby!" Fryer ordered Mike Rice to go with the woman and investigate the trouble and its cause. Following the woman to her home, he found a child about a year and a half old in a terrible condition. What little clothing it had on was torn to shreds, and the child's torso, arms and legs were badly scratched with blood freely flowing. Fortunately, the child was not fatally injured.

Back at the sheriff's office, Rice reported what he had found leading Fryer to at once order that the beast be killed. Undersheriff Hinson Thomas was delegated as the executioner, and in company with an entourage of boys he trailed the monkey to Brady's flour mill. There he located the monkey, grinning at him from the limb of a cottonwood tree. That was the monk's last earthly act. With one well-directed shot Hinson brought him to earth, ending his life but certainly not his career. When the Corrales youngsters heard of their pet's demise, their grief knew no bounds, nor did their threats of revenge on the slayers. They took the remains home intending to inter it in the local cemetery, but Gusano, the grandmother, had other ideas.

The term of the U. S. District Court was just ending, and on its adjournment Sheriff Fryer resolved to give the members of the court and bar a social send-off. As Mrs. Corrales was the acknowledged princess of Mexican cooking in Florence, famous for her tamales and enchiladas and Mexican fiestas, Sheriff Fryer ordered Mike Rice to engage Gusano to prepare a supper for twelve people and to spare no expense.

The festive evening arrived, and the layout was complete in all its details. The table actually sagged with its weight of food and beverages. As the host, Fryer occupied the place of honor at the head of the festive board. The invited guests were District Judge Joseph H. Kibbey, District Attorney Richard E. Sloan, ex-delegate to Congress Granville H. Oury, ex-sheriff A. J. Doran, Postmaster John Miller, Hon. Peter R. Brady, Sr., Undersheriff Hinson Thomas, Dan Stephens, Charley Starr, and Mike Rice. Besides the Mexican menu, the vintage liquor and cigars were of superior quality, thanks to Charley Starr's perspicacity in such matters.

The "feast of reason and flow of soul" pervaded the atmosphere. Everybody at the table vied with the others in praising Gusano's culinary artistry, but the tamales, contents of the corn shucks, was a subject of debate. Although succulent and delicious, some of the participants said that while good, they contained no chicken. Others said that it was not *carne seca,* but nobody could agree on what the tamales actually contained. Charley Starr solved the matter by his prior knowledge of Gusano's cookery. Starr said, "Gentlemen, I know what's in those corn shucks besides corn meal. Gusano has a lot of young, three-month old piggies in the back yard. She has cooked some of the porkers, and that's what's in the tamales." All finally agreed that such was the case, and discussion ceased on that point.

While the host and guests were lounging back in their chairs, telling reminiscences some of which were somewhat racy, Gusano and some of her helpers were cleaning up the deadwood in front of the banqueters. Sheriff Fryer leaned over and asked the. old lady what she had put into the tamales that made them taste so good.

She made no reply, but instead left the dining room and returned in a few minutes with her apron in her arms. Approaching the table, she emptied its contents, the head, feet and hands of the monkey, in front of the astonished guests. Indignantly, she exclaimed, "Eat it all, you sons of so-and-sos! The sheriff killed my monkey!"

Needless to say, the banqueters were less than amused. Granville Oury was especially furious, stomping out of the dining room while using the most torrid expletives and accusing the sheriff of "setting up" his guests. He never could be convinced otherwise. Kibbey, Sloan, and Doran always afterward, when chided about the "monkey tamales," strenuously denied that they partook of the tamales, but their denial was for effect. "I know," wrote Mike Rice in conclusion, "that they not only ate the monkey tamales, but they passed their plates for a second helping."

CHAPTER 7

Riverside Station

It was in a wild and remote spot in Arizona Territory, surrounded by rugged mountain ranges, just a couple of weather-beaten adobe buildings and some pole corrals near the river's ford. That could describe perhaps scores of places that no one ever heard of in Arizona, but this one was an exception.

It was on the road from Globe, the seat of Gila County, to Florence, the seat of Pinal County, and any other route between them meant traveling miles out of the way over some of the territory's roughest country. The remote spot was known as Riverside Station on the bank of the Gila River, about half-way between Globe and Florence. There traffic stopped overnight for rest, food, and red-eye whiskey, after a hard day of travel. From Globe it was over a mountain trail past places with names like Pioneer and Troy; from Florence it was over a dusty, desolate desert trail without a single human habitation of any kind.

Riverside Station was established around 1877 at the Gila crossing, near where later was the town of Kelvin, and where today is the motley collection of dwellings called Riverside. Not even ruins of the old station can be found today. It was used for over a hundred years, and was a commercial building into the 1980's when it was damaged by a flood along the Gila. Then it was torn down on the order of federal officials, no respecters of Arizona heritage, as a condition of paying one of the claims for flood damage.

It was not so much the building for which Riverside Station is remembered, however. It is for the outlaws and adventurers who took advantage of the remoteness of the station to rob the stagecoaches, hoping that the time it took to get a lawman on the trail might give them time to escape. Some of Arizona's most famous holdups, and perhaps its best-known prisoner escape, were pulled off near Riverside Station.

One of the most sensational, with far-reaching consequences, was the robbery of the Florence-Globe stagecoach on August 10, 1883, by Red Jack Elmer and his gang. In the files of the Arizona Historical Society are accounts from a newspaper, the *Arizona Enterprise* of Florence and by Sheriff A. J. Doran and Mike M.

Rice, which differ on many points, but from which the actual story can be pieced together.

Red Jack had ridden into Florence early in August, 1883, sold his horse, and seemed to be just hanging around town. When on August 10th the express box being loaded on the Globe stagecoach seemed unusually heavy, Red Jack bought a ticket on the run, saying he would board it down the street as he had to get his saddle and bridle. As the coach neared Riverside Station, Jack began to sing quite loudly, and two men rode out of a mesquite thicket, followed the coach for some distance, but before reaching the station circled around it, forded the river, and went on up the road. Later, it was found that these two had been camped in the mesquite for some days, and had been observed lounging by the side of the road, watching as the coaches passed.

The stagecoach stopped at Riverside Station so the passengers could have supper, the station then being run by men named Evans and LeBlanc. Red Jack got off and inquired whether two men had left a horse for him there. Assured they had not, Jack profanely vowed they would wish they had, and started walking along the river leaving the saddle but taking the bridle. When the stagecoach set out again on a night run to Globe, Felix LeBlanc had boarded it but Red Jack had not. It forded the river and approached the foot of the grade up the mountainside about a

The old stage station at Riverside between Globe and Florence. It was on the bank of the Gila River which flowed in the center background. The Apache Kid was a prisoner here before his escape. (Courtesy Arizona Historical Society)

mile and a half from the station. Two men opened fire on the coach without warning, killing shotgun guard Johnny Collins at the first fire with a charge of buckshot through his chin and throat. They continued to shoot, killing two of the stage horses, until driver Wat Humphrey shouted, "For God's sake, stop shooting! You have killed one man, what more do you want?" The men then emerged from their ambush and approached the stagecoach.

LeBlanc was ordered out and told to throw his money into the road, which he did. He was then told to throw down the Wells-Fargo box from the boot of the stagecoach, but it was very heavy, and Collins' body was lying atop it. The robbers told Humphrey to help LeBlanc. Humphrey asked permission to remove Collins' body, but one of the robbers said, "Let him lie where he is and get that box out now or we'll put holes through you sons of so-and-so's," whereupon by a superhuman effort LeBlanc and Humphrey dragged out the box and threw it into the road. One of the road agents handed LeBlanc a new hatchet and ordered him to break open the box. When he had done so, the robbers told LeBlanc and Humphrey to start walking up the road toward Globe, and not to return on pain of death.

The robbers then loaded one of the stage horses with the loot from the box, $2,000 in silver and $500 in gold. In their haste they overlooked $620 in currency. At the spot they had left their horses tied, they also in their haste left a pair of leather saddlebags, a belt of Winchester cartridges, an old-fashioned dirk knife, and some supplies. They left, going up the Gila River toward its confluence with the San Pedro River.

LeBlanc and Humphrey continued walking up the Globe road until they met the stagecoach coming the opposite direction, from Globe toward Riverside Station. They halted it and related what had happened. The stagecoach and passengers waited with them until morning before approaching the scene of the robbery. There they found the body of Collins still in the boot, his shotgun in the road where it had fallen when he was killed, and the box lying in the road. On turning the box over, LeBlanc found $12 of his money still lying there under it.

It was ten in the morning before word reached Florence. Sheriff A. J. Doran was at Pinal City. He received the news by telegraph, and answered back that he would meet the posse at Riverside Station. Undersheriff Lou Scanlan, Fred Adams and Mike Rice left Florence for Riverside, where they found ex-sheriff Pete Gabriel who had come in from a mining camp for supplies. Gabriel had already asked some questions about the actions of Red Jack, and determined from the answers that Jack was involved in the robbery. Charles Mason, associated with the *Enterprise* newspaper, had also arrived in Riverside from Globe, and he prepared to join the posse. When Sheriff Doran arrived, the posse set out on the trail of the murderers. At Dudleyville they learned that two men had passed through at a gallop, six-shooters in their hands, one leading a laboring pack-horse, the other behind whipping up the animal. They made no reply when loungers at the store called out, asking them why the rush. The posse also discovered that Red Jack had hired a horse, and was headed for Redfield's ranch down the San Pedro River.

The posse split up, a group proceeding down each side of the San Pedro. In one group were Pete Gabriel, Mike Rice and Charles Mason; in the other were Sheriff Doran, Undersheriff Scanlan, Fred Adams and one Harrington. Riding along the river, Gabriel picked up some twenty-dollar gold pieces dropped by the robbers, and at one point fished from the river some masks made of gunny-sack. At a small settlement called Mesaville the posse joined again, continued down the San Pedro, and obtained fresh horses from ranches they passed. At one of these they learned that Red Jack had met a man named Frank Carpenter, who gave Jack a horse. Jack continued on while Carpenter, a nephew of Len Redfield, returned to Mesaville.

"Len Redfield," wrote Mike Rice, "was well known and considered one of the most reputable citizens of Pinal County. He owned a large ranch with hundreds of cattle roaming the San Pedro valley." From the accounts, the posse split up again upon reaching Redfield's ranch, with Doran, Scanlan, Adams and Harrington camping nearby to watch developments and see that no person sneaked away during the night. Gabriel, Mason, and Rice went to the ranch house, told what their business was, and asked to stay the night. "Mr. Redfield extended a hearty welcome," continued Mike Rice, "and supper being ready led us into the dining room, ordering one of his cowboys to put up and feed our team. Many things were discussed during the evening before going to bed. The stage robbery was the principal subject. Mr. Redfield was particularly severe in denunciation of the robbers."

Before breakfast the next morning Gabriel, Mason and Rice went to the stable to throw some hay into the mangers for their horses. Mason, picking up a hay fork, stuck it into the hay pile with such force that, striking something hard in the hay, a tine snapped off. In the hay′pile they found a Wells-Fargo treasure box, containing a new hatchet which had been used to break it open. This was a great coincidence with the Riverside robbery, where the road agents used a new hatchet they later said had been given to them for the purpose of breaking open the box. They had been told to dispose of it by throwing it away, as far as they could. The Wells-Fargo box and hatchet found in Redfield's stable could only have come from a different holdup.

Gabriel, Mason and Rice were astounded at the discovery; Gabriel was speechless at such a find on the premises of one of his best friends and political supporters. He called Redfield to the stable and asked for an explanation, but Redfield had none and stoutly denied any knowledge of how the box got there. Others were then questioned, including one Joe Tuttle who lived at the ranch, but whose reputation in Globe and Florence was not of the best. From Tuttle they learned enough to implicate both Tuttle and Redfield in some suspicious activities.

Sheriff Doran and his party then arrived, and a subsequent search turned up a box containing a large amount of cash

According to George "Okie" Rutherford of Kelvin, this adobe ruin on the desert twelve miles from Riverside was Peg-leg's Station.

suspected of coming from a previous robbery near Bisbee, a U. S. mail sack, and the shotgun with which Collins had been killed at Riverside. Tuttle then made a complete confession. Redfield had been the brains behind the gang that had committed a series of robberies, and the ranch was their hideout. Tuttle and one Charles Hensley had actually staged the holdup at Riverside, Hensley having rested at the ranch a day, then moving off down the San Pedro where he was joined by Red Jack Elmer. Tuttle also confessed that the stolen silver had become so heavy and hard to transport that they had buried it temporarily in an arroyo. He was later taken under guard to the spot, and the silver was recovered.

Pete Gabriel was detached to follow the trail of Hensley and Red Jack, and the rest of the posse returned to Florence with Redfield and Tuttle under arrest. On the way it stopped and arrested Frank Carpenter at Mesaville as an accessory for furnishing the horse to Red Jack. The prisoners were all jailed in Florence where, though the whole populace was in a white heat over the robbery and murder of Collins, few still believed that Redfield had any knowledge of or connection with it. The committee of vigilantes, well-organized but which up till this time had mainly just run "undesirables" out of town, began hatching a lynching. Sheriff Doran sought out its leaders, told them he knew what they were planning, and pledged to stoutly resist any attempt to lynch the prisoners.

Len Redfield had a brother in the town of Benson near his ranch, a well-known and respected businessman. Hearing of his brother's arrest and potential danger from the vigilantes, he went to Phoenix and obtained a writ of habeas corpus for Len Redfield from Judge W. Wood Porter, in a federal court. It was given to U. S. Marshal Joe Evans to serve. When Evans arrived in Florence, Undersheriff Scanlan in the absence of Sheriff Doran refused to turn over custody of the prisoner, maintaining that the prisoners were held on a territorial, and not a federal, charge. Evans then went to Casa Grande, raised a posse of well-known hard cases, and returned. Again Scanlan refused to deliver the prisoner. While he and Evans argued in the sheriff's office, the vigilantes entered by the back door, took Redfield and Tuttle from their cells, and hanged them from the rafters in the jail corridor.

This caused an uproar in territorial legal circles, but the citizens of Florence stood on their deeds supported by most of the newspapers in the territory, and nothing was ever done about it.

The case was brought to an end, according to Sheriff Doran's reminiscences, when posses under himself and Sheriff Bob Paul of Pima County starved Red Jack and Charles Hensley, the other stage robber, out of their hideout in the Rincon Mountains near Tucson. They fled across the Sulphur Springs valley toward Willcox, coming across the camp of a freighter named Moore from whom they demanded food. Recognizing them as the wanted men, Moore told them he would put food on the tailgate of a wagon, he would leave so as not to be named as aiding and abetting criminals, and then Red Jack and Hensley could come up and get the food. Moore and his drivers sent notice to the authorities, then hid in an abandoned house nearby. When Red Jack and Hensley approached to get the food, Moore's men and the sheriff's posse opened fire on them, chased them into a nearby gulch, and killed them both.

The many accounts of the escape of the Apache Kid near Riverside Station vary widely in some respects but agree on the basic details. The Kid had one of those jaw-breaker Apache names, but earned his American name by hanging around Globe as a youth doing odd jobs. Recruited for the Apache police by the famed government scout and police superintendent Al Sieber, Kid became Sieber's trusted protege and was with him at Big Dry Wash in 1882, the last big battle between Apaches and whites. He was a veteran fighter and top sergeant when he was sent with a police detail to break up a party of Apaches, high on a native moonshine called "tulapai," which had broken out into a series of fights.

Instead of breaking up the party, Kid and his men joined in the festivities, which went on for a week with everybody getting gloriously plastered. Highly incensed, Sieber sent word to Kid to come in with his men and surrender. When Kid came in there was a shooting scrape that the Kid did not start. In the melee, Sieber was shot in the ankle and crippled for life. Sieber was very bitter and blamed the Kid for the incident. At Sieber's insistence the Kid was tried for assault with intent to kill in Globe and sentenced to Yuma penitentiary.

On November 1, 1889, Gila County Sheriff Glen Reynolds and Deputy Hunkydory Holmes set out from Globe with eight Apache prisoners in a stagecoach, and a Mexican prisoner named Jesus Avota. It was bound for Riverside Station to spend the night, from there to go to Florence and Casa Grande, and the

Portrait of Al Sieber, the famous Indian scout, taken while he still suffered from the ankle wound that crippled him for life. (Courtesy Arizona Historical Society)

The Apache Kid as a top sergeant in the Apache police and protege of Al Seiber. Found guilty of murder, the Kid and fellow criminals being taken to Yuma Prison escaped near Riverside Station. (Courtesy Arizona Historical Society)

prisoners from there by rail to Yuma. The next morning the stagecoach left Riverside Station, headed for the sandy wash in which the road ran up the bluff from the riverside to the mesa above. The Apaches now and then talked in low tones in their native tongue. Kid and another Apache wore leg irons and handcuffs, the prisoners only handcuffed. Partway up the bluffs, the stage driver, Eugene Middleton, suggested that everyone get out of the coach and walk to lighten his load. Everyone did except the Kid and the other prisoner in leg irons. Behind the coach walked Sheriff Reynolds with a shotgun, then the prisoners, with Holmes bringing up the rear with a rifle.

Some of the Apaches gradually crept forward while others held back, and at a signal they beset Reynolds and Holmes at the same time. Holmes suddenly dropped over dead. Later it was claimed from a heart attack, though his body had a bullet wound. Reynolds was shot and killed with Holmes' rifle. A bullet fired at the driver, Middleton, tore through his neck and temporarily paralyzed him, tumbling him off the box into the wash. The prisoners quickly obtained the keys from the sheriff's pockets and shed their shackles. The bodies of Reynolds and Holmes were brutally mutilated; their bodies and Middleton were stripped of everything, even clothing. Middleton, left for dead, survived.

The murderous Apaches fled the scene and scattered into the mountains. They ignored the Mexican prisoner, Avota, who cut one of the stage horses out of the traces and despite being bucked off a number of times managed to ride on into Florence where he reported the event. For this deed, Avota was pardoned of his crimes. The largest manhunt in Arizona history was mounted for the escaped Apaches, all of whom were captured or killed except the Kid, who was never again captured though he lived for many years as an outlaw in Arizona and Mexico.

The time and place of the Kid's death is unknown, though the tales of many Arizona old-timers are claims to have killed him on some foray or other. There were, however, many other renegade Apaches who never submitted to reservation life and lived in the wild subsisting by hunting and thievery.

The best clue to the Kid's death may have been a report of a fight with Apaches by troops of Old Mexico. An Apache band was found entering that country from the States, and in a sharp fight with the Mexican soldiers, some of the Indians were killed.

Since one Apache was the same as another to the Mexicans, the bodies were left where they fell. From one of the dead, however, a gold watch inscribed with Glen Reynolds' name and a large amount of American greenbacks were taken. As Reynolds was carrying a large amount of money when he was killed, in all probability the slain Apache who was carrying the watch and the money was the Apache Kid.

Accounts of a holdup by King Ussery of a stagecoach near Riverside on January 5th, 1892, again agree in the essentials but vary in some other respects. Ussery had a farm on the Salt River, and also ran cattle in the Tonto Basin and on some of the hills along the Salt near Usery Pass northeast of Mesa, "Usery" being a corruption of the name "Ussery." On that January day, however, he and an acquaintance named Henry Blevins decided to dabble in stagecoach robbery. They leaped out of the brush as the coach ascended the bluffs near Riverside Station, and surprised the driver, Jack Goff. They looted the load, taking two silver bars valued at $1,500 each, and other booty worth a few hundred dollars more, told Goff to take off and keep going, and fired their guns in the air.

While Ussery and Blevins headed back toward the Salt River settlements, Goff was reporting the robbery to Sheriff J. H. Thompson at Globe. The driver had thought he recognized one of the bandits, and with other clues at hand, Thompson started to the Tonto Basin to question Ussery. Some accounts say that on the way he met a Salt River rancher who said that he had seen a man answering Ussery's description acting suspiciously and digging a hole as if to bury something, and, following this lead, Thompson recovered a bar of silver. Other accounts are that Thompson followed tracks to the bank of the Salt River. Where a cottonwood log had fallen and extended out over the river, Thompson noticed a piece of barbed wire dragged in the water, and blood stains on the wire. Pulling on the wire fished the silver bar out of the river.

Reports of the disposition of this case also vary, one being that Ussery was tried and found guilty in Globe, sentenced to seven years in Yuma territorial prison but pardoned two years later, and that Blevins was never apprehended nor the other silver bar found. Another is that both Ussery and Blevins were tried in Florence, with Ussery being convicted but Blevins found not guilty.

In another stagecoach robbery near Riverside Station the featured crook was Pearl Hart, the notorious female bandit, a fact that got her nationwide attention on the front pages. That was particularly true of Arizona newspapers, all of which produced reams of stories on the robbery and on Pearl in particular. All of this led to many versions over the years, including one in a magazine from an interview given by Pearl herself. The conflicting tales make it difficult to get an accurate picture of her life before the holdup, the robbery itself, and its aftermath.

Born in Canada, Pearl was 27 years old when she first arrived in Phoenix in 1898. According to her story, when the husband who had deserted her twice did so again, she left Phoenix and was on her own. She obtained work as a cook in the mining town of Mammoth, where she lived in a tent on the bank of the Gila River. This life proved to be too hard, so she packed her possessions in a wagon, intending to move to Globe. A man named Joe Boot who had some mining claims nearby wanted to go to Globe, too, so they paid eight dollars to have their wagons freighted to that city. There Pearl went to work in a miners' boarding house, but one of the big mines closed and she was out of a job. She went with Joe Boot to his mining claims and helped work them, but the claims were poor, they ran out of money, and had to give it up.

That is the type of story Pearl could be expected to maintain, though there is one that is less virtuous in tone. That is that the tent she occupied near Mammoth was in the company of another girl, and that their feminine charms made easy prey of the rough-and-ready miners. Joe Boot was a tin-horn gambler in the mining camp who aided the girls in their enterprise and profited from it also. When mining at the Mammoth began to diminish, so did the girls' business, and Pearl's partner opted for greener pastures, leaving Pearl and Joe in bad straits. In either case, it may be deduced that Pearl was a lady of easy virtue who did not hesitate to use her femaleness whenever the occasion demanded.

Pearl's story was that she received word that her mother was ill and she needed money hurriedly to return to her mother's side. True or not, she and Joe decided it was time to shake off the Arizona dust and the quickest way to finance such a move was to rob a stagecoach. So, late in the afternoon of May 30, 1899, as the Florence-Globe stagecoach was passing Cane Springs near Riverside Station, two masked figures jumped from the chaparral with drawn guns and ordered the driver to halt. Though the

Pearl Hart, the notorious female outlaw, poses in the yard of the old Pinal County Courthouse after her capture by a posse under Sheriff William Truman, background. (Courtesy Arizona Historical Society)

bandanas covered their lower faces and both were wearing men's clothing, it was evident that one of them was a woman. The passengers were ordered out into the road, and while most accounts say Pearl held a .38 on them while Joe robbed them, Pearl's is that Joe held a .45 on the passengers while Pearl did the honors — and after all, she was an eye-witness.

"Joe told me to search the passengers for arms," goes her story. "I carefully went through them all. They had no pistols. Joe motioned toward the stage. I advanced and searched it, and found the brave passengers had left two of their guns behind them when ordered out of the stage . . . I gave Joe a .44 and kept the .45 for myself. Joe told me to search the passengers for money. I did so, and found on the fellow who was shaking the worst $390. The fellow was trembling so I could hardly get my hand in his pockets. The other fellow, a sort of a dude with his hair parted in the middle, tried to tell me how much he needed the money, but he yielded $36, a dime and two nickels. Then I searched the Chinaman. He was nearer my size and I just scared him to death. His clothing enabled me to go through him quickly, I only got five dollars, however. The stage driver had a few dollars, but after a council of war we decided not to rob him. Then we gave each of the others a charitable contribution of a dollar apiece and ordered them to move on, warning them not to look back if they valued their lives." Pearl and Joe also kept a gold watch.

For the next few hours Pearl and Joe rode aimlessly through the mountains, in an attempt to confuse the posse they knew would be on their trail. They even came back past Riverside Station before setting out along the San Pedro River toward Benson where they hoped to catch a train eastward. No planning for the escape had been made, Joe Boot even had to chance going into a Mammoth store for food. They found a cave in which they planned to sleep, but found it occupied by a javelina, or wild pig, which Joe shot before it charged them. They traveled all of the final night of their freedom and then, exhausted, lay down to sleep. They did not know that they were only twenty miles from Benson, their destination.

Pearl and Joe were wakened by Pinal County Sheriff William C. Truman's posse, which took them back to Florence where they were thrown into the pokey to await trial. The press and public had a field day with Pearl, who became a great curiosity. She posed for pictures wearing and carrying guns. It was reported that her sister, an actress, had written a play for her entitled "Arizona Bandit" in which Pearl would star. She even made sure someone saw her swallowing a dose of a mysterious powder, whereupon the doctor was summoned and pronounced the "suicide" attempt a hoax.

Having no facilities for women in his Pinal County jail, Sheriff Truman took her to Tucson, where she was lodged in a room with no bars, only lath and plaster walls. One morning there was a hole in the wall of the room, and Pearl was missing, along with a trusty named Ed Hogan. Ed was a small-time thief; one Tucson newspaper stated that " . . . he is in reality one Sherwood, the notorious Phoenix bicycle thief."

Pearl was recaptured in Deming, New Mexico, by Deputy Sheriff George Scarborough, himself a gun fighter of some note. Pearl was returned to Tucson and Ed Hogan disappeared. Perhaps no one even looked for him.

Pearl and Joe Boot were tried in Florence in November, 1899, for stage robbery before Judge Fletcher M. Doan and a twelve-man jury. To the amazement of Judge Doan and the outrage of the citizenry, the jury brought in a verdict of "not guilty." The judge had no choice but to dismiss the jury, but not before he had given them a fearful tongue-lashing and barred them from the jury panel for the rest of the court session. Pearl and Joe were promptly re-arrested on a charge of interfering with the U. S. mails, and tossed into the Tucson slammer to await trial again. This time they were convicted; Pearl got five years in Yuma Prison, while Joe drew a thirty-year rap.

After two years Joe Boot escaped from the Yuma Penitentiary and was never heard from again. Three years after her conviction, in December, 1902, Governor Alexander Brodie, to the consternation once more of the populace, pardoned Pearl Hart with the condition that she leave Arizona immediately and not return during the term of her sentence. Later on, it was claimed that Brodie's reason for the pardon was that Pearl had convinced him she was pregnant, and the governor was unwilling to face the scandal and political consequences of her claim should it prove to be true.

Doubtless there were other stagecoach holdups and robberies along the Globe-Florence road and near Riverside Station in those lawless days, if only the pioneers could tell us about them from their graves, or lost files of old newspapers be found and examined. The country around Riverside Station, once enlivened by great copper strikes in the hills, is gradually fading back into rustic peace and quiet because of the ills of the copper industry. The towns of Ray, Sonora, and Barcelona have come and gone, swallowed up in a great open pit copper mine. Superior and Kelvin are languishing, Hayden and the new town of Kearney are still getting along. Winkelman and Dudleyville, cowtowns of the Old West, have not changed much for many years.

The old road from Globe to Riverside Station can now be traveled only with great difficulty. Stretches of it have long been abandoned. The lonely reaches of the Florence to Riverside road are still traveled, but it is a well-maintained county road now, wide, graded and graveled rather than the narrow, rutted, dusty desert trail it once was. It still switchbacks up the bluff from the Gila River, near where in the desert wash the Apache Kid made his escape. And at the riverside, the old station has been forced to give up the ghost, along with the pioneers, good and bad, who once sought its shelter.

Should you want to visit the site of old Riverside Station, it is a pleasant and scenic trip. From U. S. highway 89 in Florence, turn off to pass in front of the main gate of today's state prison. This street leads you to the desert road, where you drive the thirty miles to Riverside through the cactus forest. Alternatively, travelers may leave U. S. highway 60 at Superior, turning southeasterly on Arizona highway 177 toward Hayden and Kearney. The paved road runs past the vast open pit copper mine and descends into the Mineral Creek canyon. At its bottom is a sign denoting the turn-off to Riverside and Florence, and down the road a short distance is the Gila River bridge. From either direction, turn in to Riverside on the paved road and follow it to the pavement's end. Straight ahead about a hundred yards on the left is the site of the old station. It is rubble-strewn, surrounded by a brokendown fence, and sparse shade trees. No one else may be there, but you are not alone. The spirits of Sheriffs Glen Reynolds, Jim Doran and Bill Truman, and of Red Mike, Pearl Hart and the Apache Kid still whisper to you of their deeds of long ago.

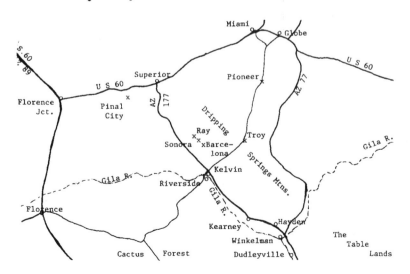

CHAPTER 8
Arizona Characters

Anyone who delves into the history of Arizona Territory soon is struck by the variety of colorful characters who inhabited it. That's because Arizona was one of the last of the states to be formed; its history is comparatively recent. Historical societies were organized early, and the pioneers who lived through the frontier era urged to write down their life experiences to be preserved in the societies' files.

Now, along with the official record of the monumental events in Arizona history and the day-to-day accounts of life in Arizona's towns found in microfilmed newspaper files, there are also the personal histories of the pioneer men and women who lived in those towns and shaped those events. Unfortunately, some of the most fascinating are the fragmentary references to people who did not leave a personal history, to be found in the stories of those who did.

Take, for instance, the references to one Dave Gibson. Probably he was not considered important enough to be invited to join a historical society. Was he a stage driver, the "D. Gibson" of reference in Chapter 1 of this book whose coach was late arriving at Agua Fria Station? Nothing else tells whether he was a cowboy, a laborer, or merely a saloon lounger and drifter. Yet, where there were incidents of violence Dave Gibson was there, mentioned by those who did set down the accounts.

The reminiscenses of John F. Crampton who lived and worked at Maricopa Wells stage station mention Gibson. In 1880 one of the stations on the overland trail along the Gila River between Maricopa Wells and Yuma was called Mission camp. It had been established on the site of an abandoned Spanish mission, probably that founded by Father Kino in the eighteenth century. Early in December, 1870, the station was sold by John Kilbright to Peter Reed who moved there with his wife. On December 24th the station was attacked by Mexican bandits. They had killed Reed and the hostler, chopped off the head of the cook, Thomas Oliver, with an axe, and had Mrs. Reed by the hair of her head when an inspection party arrived and frightened the bandits away, saving Mrs. Reed's life. In the inspection party were the superintendent of the stage line, James A. Moore, his son-in-law to be, Charles A. Kenyon, a Col. Hinton, and Dave Gibson.

Elsewhere in this book is the description of events one night in August, 1887, when jailor Mike Rice found himself the only representative of the law present in the town of Florence. The sheriff and all his deputies were out of town. Rice received a tip that vigilantes were secretly meeting, planning to storm the jail and lynch the prisoners being held there for murder. Rice could recruit only half a dozen people on short notice to help him hold the jail against the expected vigilante raid. One of them was Dave Gibson.

"I called on Dave Gibson and persuaded him to help me hold the prisoners," wrote Rice. " . . . I met Gibson at the sheriff's office and got for him a sawed-off shotgun loaded with buckshot . . . I stationed Gibson in a vacant room across the narrow street fronting the jail." Fortunately, the vigilantes dispersed when confronted by Rice and his defenders, and Gibson did not have to shoot.

The classic gun duel between Pete Gabriel and Joe Phy, which took place in Florence on May 31, 1888, is also described elsewhere in this book. Again Dave Gibson was there. Joe Phy, shot through, staggered out of the Tunnel Saloon and fell across the sidewalk. The accounts are that Dave Gibson bent over Phy and asked, "Joe, are you hurt much?" Phy, holding his gun in one hand and a razor-sharp knife in the other, replied "Go away from me, you murdering _____ ," at the same time slashing at Gibson with the knife, cutting his leg to the bone just above the knee.

Phy's dying reference to Dave Gibson as a murderer may be explained by another violent incident in which Gibson was involved, recorded by Mike Rice. This event occurred some months before the Gabriel-Phy gun battle, but Rice did not mention the date. "(Pete Gabriel) and I were both in Tucson registered at the Cosmopolitan Hotel the night of the killing of Jim Levy (real name James Dunleavy) by Johnny Murphy, (William) Moyer, and Dave Gibson. Murphy and Levy quarreled over a gambling issue, and it was agreed . . . that they should fight a duel. Teams were hired at Ed Bullock's livery stable to carry the principals and their seconds to some point out of town where the fight was to be staged. City Marshal Buttner, hearing of the arrangements, determined to prevent the fight. He chased all over town trying to find Murphy and Levy and disarm them. He met Levy on the church plaza and took away his gun. He failed to locate Murphy, nor did he see him until the moment of his arrest immediately after the tragedy.

"Considerable excitement prevailed in the resorts (saloons) over the forthcoming affair. Gabriel was a warm friend to Murphy and tried to use his influence with him to stop the meeting. Although (Gabriel) was unacquainted with Levy, he knew his reputation as a gun-fighter and believed Murphy would not have a chance against his opponent. Many peacemakers and advisers butted into the affair, only aggravating the matter into a deeper intensity. One man, Matt Reading, told Johnny Murphy in my own hearing that he was about to commit suicide by confronting Levy in a gun battle. He said, 'Johnny, Levy can give you the first shot and then shoot the buttons off your vest.' This did not deter Murphy in the least; what he lacked in marksmanship, he made up for it in courage and nerve.

"Many friends of Levy assumed that Marshal Buttner deliberately permitted Murphy to retain his gun, an unjust aspersion, as no man who ever wore an official badge in Tucson ever topped him as an efficient and dependable law officer. But, if Jim Levy had been armed that night, another episode would have been written, and many of his assailants would have bitten the dust. Moyer admitted to me (Rice) years after in Alaska that fear of Levy's deadly aim brought about his death. They knew this, hence they took no chances.

" . . . On the porch of the Cosmopolitan Hotel, Gabriel called me aside and said, 'Mike, let's go uptown and locate Murphy and Dave Gibson. I believe I can stop this damned nonsense.' I replied, 'Pete, it is none of my pie. I don't want to be mixed up in their affairs.' He then said, 'What's the matter with you? Are you afraid?' to which I replied 'If you put it that way, no, they have always been friendly to me.' We started up Pennington Street, crossed through the alley toward the Palace Hotel on Myers Street, and there saw Johnny Murphy and Dave Gibson on the opposite sidewalk. Gabriel hailed Murphy but received no reply. They crossed the street toward the hotel entrance. Gabriel caught my arm and pulled me into the shelter of a boot-black stand about ten feet from the hotel door.

"Murphy and Gibson, as soon as they reached the door, met

Levy coming from the office and instantly a fusillade of shots belched from their revolvers into Levy's body. This did not bring him down at the moment. He passed his assailants staggering, with uplifted arms, crying 'I am unarmed, you cowardly __ of ____ !', moved forward a few paces, and dropped dead near the opposite sidewalk. A crowd assembled around the prostrate form. In a few minutes Dr. Handy arrived and after a brief examination of the body pronounced Levy dead. Here Dave Gibson, bareheaded and in short sleeves, his arms waving in the air howled out, 'Doctor, bring him a box! He got just what was coming to him!'

"I saw the victim's body during the inquest and his torso was literally punctured with bullets. If I remember rightly, twelve bullets pierced his body. After Levy fell to the street, . . . flashes of fire (came) from an apparent arsenal in the doorways opposite the hotel. It was later learned that 'Crooked-mouth' Green was one of the concealed assassins, yet this cowardly scoundrel was never arrested or brought to justice. He dropped completely from sight.

"I (Mike Rice) was a witness for the prosecution at Moyer's trial. He was the only man convicted. Murphy and Gibson, after many delays, were acquitted. All three of them escaped from the county jail and were fugitives for many months. Moyer was captured in Denver, and Murphy and Gibson were captured out in Death Valley country, by either Sheriff Bob Paul or Sheriff Bob Leatherwood, who ran them to earth. Gabriel avoided subpoena as a witness by (fleeing) beyond the court's jurisdiction, reversing his usual stand in this case by putting friendship first before duty."

The reminiscences of Mike Rice, pioneer newspaperman and sometimes law officer, also describe an irascible though less violent character named W. M. Stewart. "Mickey Stewart, the 'Father of Coconino County,' wrote Rice, "was a character unduplicatable, an unexplainable paradox, aggressive, combative, conciliatory, suave, yet subtle . . . He was a man of small stature, weight about 130 pounds, with flaming red hair, and he would fight a buzz-saw if provoked. He feared neither god, dean or devil . . . The nickname 'Mickey' was bestowed upon him by his Flagstaff friends and he prided himself on the appellation."

Stewart arrived in Flagstaff from parts unknown, obtained a clerical job, and soon came to public notice as a member of the Council for Yavapai County, which at that time included all of what is now Coconino County. Stewart more than any other individual was responsible for the ultimate separation of Coconino County from Yavapai, to the exasperation of the Yavapai delegation to the legislature. The Prescott people did not want to lose Coconino's valuable political and business assets, and threatened Stewart with political oblivion if he persisted. Stewart, however, would not be denied and finally was successful in his mission.

"He was in constant turmoil with his fellow legislators," wrote Rice, "both vocally and physically. His combats ranged far afield from the territorial capital and his fracases were many." He remained popular enough with his Republican party that eventually it made him its candidate for Arizona delegate to the U. S. House of Representatives.

Stewart was embroiled in a bitter battle in the legislature over the territorial printing bill with Tom Weedin of Pinal County. One day, walking to the Prescott post office with Colonel Bridwell of Graham County and Mike Rice, Weedin came upon Stewart coming out of a saloon and plastered to the gills. "Stewart violently assailed Weedin, using the most foul and fighting language, and abusing him in the most violent terms," said Rice, but Weedin ignored him and passed on. Enraged, Stewart seized a three-foot wrench from the hands of a fireman adjusting a hydrant, rushed up behind Weedin, and raised it to bash him in the back of the head."

"Look out, Tom!" shouted Rice, who leaped between the two men and took the blow glancing off his shoulder and arm. Bridwell grabbed the wrench away from Stewart, who would have killed Weedin had the blow landed. "Later Stewart made a most sincere apology," recalled Mike Rice, "which was as sincerely accepted by Weedin, and the incident was closed by deep libations at a nearby bar. The two former enemies were thereafter the closest of personal friends."

Another incident involving Stewart near Phoenix was also recorded by Mike Rice. "Meeting Mickey in the bar of the Commercial Hotel," he wrote, "and after an irrigating ceremony (getting sloshed), Mickey invited me to join him in a buggy ride to Tempe, where he had an appointment with Governor Zulick . . . Along the way and when passing directly in front of the entrance to the insane asylum (at 24th and Van Buren Streets) we met a man from Flagstaff named Fitzpatrick, the former husband of Stewart's wife. They both reined up their horses, and Stewart passing the reins to me nimbly jumped from the buggy. Fitzpatrick also jumped to the ground, and without a word from either of them there occurred about as lively a scrap as I ever witnessed . . ."

Fitzpatrick, a raw-boned six-footer, was handy with his fists, and the 130-pound Mickey bounced against him like a rubber ball. He was decked several times during the battle that went on until both combatants were completely exhausted. "Stewart got the worst of it," said Rice, "but he would not admit defeat. His face was badly lacerated and one of his eyes was completely closed . . . The affair (was) also witnessed by a bunch of inmates, male and female, who were hanging on the fence enclosing the asylum, hilariously enjoying the combat." Stewart made Rice promise to say that the team had shied and thrown Stewart into a cat-claw thicket, which explanation was designed to keep the details from newspaper reporters and saloon scandal-mongers. Evidently Fitzpatrick also wanted it hushed up, so no public report was ever made.

"Soon after this event," continued Rice, "I personally carried Mickey Stewart in my arms down the stairway of the Commercial Hotel and out to a waiting carriage, accompanied him to the railroad depot, and saw him on the train for his last ride to Flagstaff . . . Shortly after his return to Flagstaff he succumbed to that dread disease, tuberculosis. He was attended by Dr. Brennan, physician for the Santa Fe Company, who reported to me Stewart's last words. Brennan told Stewart he was near death and asked if he desired spiritual consolation. Stewart replied, "Well, doctor, if God Almighty has nothing better to do than trying to make an angel out of Mickey Stewart I have no complaint to make. I resign to the inevitable." And the emaciated mortal turned his face to the wall and his spirit passed into the eternal void." Then Mike Rice added, revealingly, "This is (sugar) coated as to Stewart's last words on earth."

The reminiscences of Arizona pioneer George Gamble, who arrived in Clifton in 1893, described two colorful characters who also played out some of their part on the Arizona stage in that town. One was known as "Cyclone Bill," though before his Arizona days he had been known as W. E. (Abe) Beck. Having studied law as a young man in Texas and been admitted to the bar, he formed a partnership with another young lawyer and opened an office at the first term of court. A fellow charged with stealing cattle was asked by the judge if he had a lawyer. The prisoner said that he didn't have the money to hire one, so the judge said, "I will appoint Abe Beck and his partner to defend you." The prisoner looked at the two young lawyers and inquired if that was them. "Yes, both of them," replied the judge. The prisoner said, "I plead guilty." Cyclone Bill said he immediately walked out of the courthouse, went to punching cattle, and never tried to practice law any more.

Cyclone Bill had been all over the territory before arriving in Clifton and was known by practically everyone, especially the residents of the Gila valley. An unusual man in many respects, he was splendidly equipped mentally. He was above average height, but had been crippled in the left knee, according to him, from a gunshot wound. He limped badly, as one leg was short and stiff, and he sometimes stood upright on the good leg while at others resting on the short leg, at which time he appeared to be a very short man.

Unable to do hard labor because of the leg, he had to live by his wits and there is no report that he ever went hungry. He first gained wide notoriety by being arrested as implicated in the famous Wham army payroll robbery at Cedar Springs, but proved an alibi and was released. It was after this incident that Cyclone Bill went to Clifton.

One story about him is that he entered a bar where a new bartender was on duty who had never been introduced to Cyclone Bill. Bill approached the bar while the bartender was busy with other customers and stood down on his short leg. When the bartender got around to asking him what he wanted, Bill ordered drinks for the house. While the drinks were being served and the bartender's back was turned, Cyclone Bill stepped away from the bar and stood tall on his good leg. The bartender looked all around, not recognizing him, and asked where that little son-of-a-gun was who had ordered the drinks.

Another incident in a saloon happened in Solomonville while the well-known Judge Fletcher M. Doan was holding court there. An old friend from civilized country was visiting the judge and had attended the afternoon session of court. The way to their hotel led by the Palace Saloon, and the judge and his friend stopped in for a cold soda water. Cyclone Bill happened to be in the place, and the judge, wishing to point out all the attractions of the West, introduced his friend to Cyclone Bill.

Bill stretched himself up to his extreme height, and in towering wrath, said "I will give you to understand, sir, that my name is W. E. Beck." The judge apologized and said, "Oh, yes, I know who you are, Mr. Beck, but as you are popularly known as Cyclone Bill I didn't suppose you would object to being introduced as such." Cyclone retorted, "You are popularly known around here as a first class ___ ___ ___, but I don't think you would want to be introduced as such."

One Saturday night Cyclone Bill hit up Joe Reaves, bartender at the Blue Goose Saloon, for a loan of five dollars. Joe, knowing Cyclone, hesitated, but Bill assured him that he had some money coming to him, that he would get it on Monday morning, and Joe would be repaid. "If I'm alive, you'll get your money Monday morning," promised Bill, and Joe coughed up the five. Next Monday morning, Cyclone Bill had not showed up, and Joe Reaves was sitting in the doorway of the Blue Goose, getting some sun. An acquaintance happened by and asked the usual question, "What's new today?" Joe replied, "Well, Cyclone Bill is dead."

Cyclone Bill ran for justice of the peace in Clifton against a very worthy man named Abe Boyles. The sporting crowd, gamblers and saloon loungers, put up Cyclone Bill as a joke, and many jokingly voted for him. When the votes were counted, it appeared that Bill had gotten most of them, but the election board threw out thirteen ballots as being improperly marked. Bill not being the regular nominee, his name had to be written in, and of the thirteen, one was marked Cyclone, one was marked Tornado William, and the other eleven Cyclone Bill. These thirteen ballots having been thrown out, Boyles won the election by three votes.

At that time there was a law on the books stating that any precinct having 5,000 or more inhabitants was entitled to two sets of precinct officers. Cyclone Bill got busy, took his own census of the precinct, found that there were the required number of people, and declared that he was entitled to be a justice of the peace. He opened up an office and proceeded to hold court. The supervisors refused to issue a certificate on the grounds that the census was not official, so when the court ruled against him Bill stepped down from the bench.

According to Mr. Gamble, Cyclone Bill's own version of how he came by that name is the best of the many that once floated around. When the Southern Pacific railroad reached Yuma, building eastward, there was a big business freighting supplies to Tucson and other points. Freighting was done mostly by mule teams, and Bill met an acquaintance in Yuma who had a fine ten-mule team. He wanted someone to handle the team for a share of the profits, which were big, as the Apaches were on the warpath and the owner was putting up his outfit against the driver's life. Cyclone took the job but never arrived in Tucson with the outfit.

After a year had passed Cyclone Bill ventured into Tucson, and about the first person he met was the owner of the freight outfit. He demanded the team and an explanation of the whole affair. Cyclone told him that when he had gotten out on the road, about half-way to Tucson, a cyclone came upon him, gathered the team, load, and himself all up in the sky, and whirled them away through space. He didn't have any idea where he lit upon the earth, but as he remembered the direction the cyclone was traveling when it struck him, he started to walk back to Tucson, he walked continuously, and had just then arrived in Tucson.

The other character of Gamble's reminiscence was a young man raised in Washington, DC, as Rufus Nephews, but came West and got a job punching cattle in the northern part of Arizona. He used such an astonishing amount of Climax chewing tobacco that the cowboys called him "Climax Jim." After acquiring some knowledge of how to handle range cattle, the possibilities of one aspect of it occurred to him, and he entered the business on his own hook — and without a ranch. He had varied success, because the owners of the cattle he handled often interfered with his activities, with the result that he frequently landed in jail.

As a business adjunct, he acquired a specialized knowledge of lockpicking, specializing in jail doors, handcuffs and leg irons. He boasted that he had escaped from every pen in the territory except the territorial prison at Yuma. He said he didn't like the way they treated fellows who tried to escape, and as he had only a year to serve there, he didn't try. When Ben Clark was sheriff of Graham County, Climax Jim worked the combination of the jail door and escaped, disarmed the jailor and tied and gagged him. After locking the man in the cell, Jim escaped with seven other prisoners, leaving only one who chose to stay in the jail. The sheriff, however, then out-guessed the escapees' plans and recaptured them at a place called Ash Flat.

"When the Forbes store in Clifton was broken into," recalled Gamble, "and the money along with some merchandise was taken, suspicion was directed to Climax Jim because of his known ability to open locks. Officers searched his premises but found nothing. "Hard Times Porko" was deputy sheriff and "Jake" Sailers was constable. There was a shallow well in Climax's yard which looked as though loose sand had been dumped into it. So, the officers got a shovel and started to dig. Climax said, on account of the hard work required to shovel out the loose sand, he didn't worry about it at first, thinking they would not dig long. But when the officers showed so much unexpected endurance and tenacity, he began to get interested. It was a very hot day, the work was very strenuous, and they finally gave it up. Climax said that because of the extreme heat and the hard work of the officers, he (Climax Jim) himself was wringing wet with sweat when they gave it up."

The Bank of Morenci once forwarded a bunch of pay checks to the Clifton bank to be returned to the Arizona Copper Company, but the cancelled checks didn't reach the Clifton bank, presumably having been stolen from the post office. Climax Jim was caught trying to pass one of the paid checks — the paid stamp having been removed. The trial came up at Solomonville, and the district attorney solemnly rose to offer the check in evidence as Exhibit Number 1 for the prosecution. Carefully, he laid it on the table at his side. Climax Jim, who was sitting nearby with his attorney, at a propitious moment reached over, got the check, chewed it up and swallowed it. When the attorney reached over for it, the check was gone and so was his case, dismissed for lack of evidence.

On another occasion, Climax was indicted for rustling cattle in Graham County. When the trial came up, he had witnesses to prove that the offense was not committed in Graham County, but that it was in Apache County, and so he was acquitted. Promptly re-arrested and indicted in Apache County for stealing the same cattle, he produced witnesses to prove that the theft occurred not in Apache County but in Graham County, and he was acquitted again.

CHAPTER 9

Jewel of the Arizona Desert

Today's surprise quiz question, class, is "What Arizona city was once a wild west town started by a collection of adventurers, opportunists and wanderers, with a few industrious citizens and settlers thrown in as a glue to hold it all together?" See if you can come up with the answer on your first guess.

Tombstone, you say? Nope. Clifton? Wrong again. The correct answer is Phoenix, the modern jewel of the Arizona desert. But don't be taken in by all of the asphalt, concrete, steel, glass, glitz, blurb and hype. It is all a mirage. Phoenix, while never as wild as Tombstone or Clifton, was once a wide-open Western town. There were gunfights, stagecoach hold-ups, jail-deliveries and lynchings. We won't even mention murder; it is more common now than it was then, only in frontier Phoenix murderers didn't get away with it.

Phoenix owes its existence to the establishment of Fort McDowell, a military outpost, in September, 1865. It was on the Verde River, seven miles north of its junction with the Salt River, northeast of the Valley of the Sun. The Civil War ended that year, troops were sent west again to put a stop to Indian depredations and make the land safe for settlers. Only traces of the old fort remain now, part of an adobe officers' quarters, a stone chapel built after the fort was decommissioned, and a cemetery where rest the old Indian scouts who guided army patrols. When it was first built, however, McDowell and its satellite post, Camp Reno on the banks of Tonto Creek to the northeast, were important stations. From them the cavalry and infantry sallied forth north along the Verde, into the Tonto Basin, and the Superstition and Pinal Mountain ranges to wrest control of the land from the Apaches.

Supplying food for the soldiers and their horses and mules was the duty of army quartermasters who let contracts to civilian suppliers for beef, food crops, hay and barley. The army also contracted with civilians to operate stores at army posts where soldiers and attached civilians could buy non-army-issue goods.

The store keepers were called "sutlers." Many discharged army men and former sutlers took up contracts to furnish supplies to McDowell and Reno, and became prominent in the founding of

Arizona pioneer Jack Swilling. Note gun in right hand, resting on his shoulder. Cut from the original picture in which his Indian adopted son appeared at his left. (Courtesy Arizona Historical Society)

Phoenix and nearby communities. Two of these men were John Y. T. Smith who established a hay camp on the bank of the Salt River near Phoenix, and W. B. Hellings (or Helling) who later built a flour mill near what is now 32nd and Van Buren Streets in Phoenix.

Areas along the Salt River for miles were then dotted with the ruins of ancient Indian pueblos and communities. The valley floor was lined with their ancient irrigation ditches, hand-dug for miles, by Indians who watered their crops from the Salt River. The Indians had abandoned it all centuries ago.

In 1867, a man named Jack Swilling of Wickenburg visited John Smith at his hay camp east of Phoenix near what is now the preserved Pueblo Grande ruin. He took in the stories of profits to be made by raising and selling hay and grain crops to the Army, and looked over the miles of abandoned irrigation ditches stretching across the level valley, just waiting for someone to put them back into service. Swilling returned to Wickenburg excited over the prospect, and on September 18, 1867, a meeting was held there at which the Swilling Irrigating Canal Company was organized with a capital of $10,000.

(For most of the Phoenix story to follow we are indebted to the famed Arizona historian, James H. McClintock, whose references and materials are preserved in the Phoenix public library.)

Early in December, 1867, the company of workers who were to restore the old canals and reclaim the farms from the desert left Wickenburg with its wagon train of supplies, tools, and draft animals. That many of them were drifters and adventurers cannot be denied. Their names were listed as Peter Burnes, one Chapman, Jacob Denslinger, B. P. Darrell Duppa, Thomas J. L. Hogue, John Larsen, James Lee, Thomas McGoldrick, Michael McGrath, Thomas McWilliams, Frank S. Metzler, Antonio Moreas, James Smith, John W. Swilling, Lovedick Vandemark, P. S. Walters, and Joseph Woods.

Only two of them have ever been heard of again. Volumes have been written about those two, Jack Swilling and Darrell Duppa. If ever two men could be termed wanderers and adventurers, it was they.

Swilling was a South Carolinian born in 1830 who drifted west and was working for the Butterfield Overland Stage line. Then, placer gold was discovered at Gila City on the line in Arizona, a few miles east of the present Yuma, in 1858. Swilling joined the gold rush to Gila City, along with a thousand or more others, but the gold played out in a few short months. Some para-military groups were then being formed to fight marauding Indian bands, and Swilling joined one pursuing Yavapai Indians north along the Hassayampa River. He left it to go to Pinos Altos, New Mexico, where he joined another such para-military group. When the Civil War broke out, Swilling's outfit and other such bands were impressed into the Confederate army.

They were under the command of Confederate Colonel John R. Baylor of Texas who sent Capt. Sherod Hunter with a hundred men westward along the old Butterfield trail to Tucson to secure Arizona for the confederacy. Swilling was in Hunter's force, but did not, as some have claimed, fight in the only battle of the Civil War in Arizona, near the Picacho Peak. Prior to that fight, scouts of the Confederate force had surprised and captured an advance force of the Union's eastward-bound California Column at the Pima village of Casa Blanca. The captured Union soldiers were paroled at Tucson except for their commander, Capt. William McCleave. Swilling was one of those transporting McCleave back to New Mexico as a prisoner of war at the time of the Picacho skirmish.

The men who had been impressed into service with the Confederates never had considered themselves part of the army, as they were forced to join it, and therefore felt free to leave it whenever they chose. That's what Swilling did shortly after returning to New Mexico, causing some to label him later as a deserter from the Southern army.

Back in Arizona in 1863, he joined the famous Peeples Expedition into central Arizona, guided by the well-known scout and mountain man, Pauline Weaver, to search for gold. According to Peeples, Swilling was not in the original party departing from Yuma, but joined it after it had discovered gold at Rich Hill or Antelope Hill. He had wandered to Wickenburg by 1867, when he visited John Smith's hay camp.

A rough and tough frontiersman, Swilling was a violent man, and especially so on one of his frequent drunken sprees. Unconfirmed stories say he left South Carolina after killing a man in a duel, killed eleven men in Kansas in retaliation for the murder of his uncle, killed another man who attacked him in California, and still another in Arizona shortly after his arrival, an army officer who attempted to take a gun away from him. It was also claimed that one day in Wickenburg he became angry over some incident and killed three Mexicans, scalped them, and for a time wore the scalps dangling from his belt. His wife, Trinidad, he had married in Tucson when she was seventeen years of age. They had five children, and Swilling also adopted an Indian boy who had been captured in a raid on an Apache camp.

After his Phoenix experiences, of which more will presently be told, Swilling returned to the Agua Fria River country, north of Phoenix. Near today's Black Canyon City he farmed, ranched, prospected, and dealt in mining properties. Because of a back injury which constantly troubled him, he had turned to morphine to ease the pain, and had become addicted. Like other prominent but controversial men (Wyatt Earp was another), he had a host of stout friends and defenders as well as many detractors who never excused some of his actions and to whom he was "Swilling the notorious."

Swilling was often in the town of Gillett, on the Agua Fria River below the Tiptop Mine in the Bradshaw Mountains. It was named for the mine's superintendent, Dan Gillett, and location of the mine's ore mill. Arriving there one day, Swilling was drinking in a saloon. A few days before, there had been a stagecoach robbery on the Phoenix-Prescott route, when a man was killed and some gold coins taken. Swilling jokingly boasted of robbing the stage, and produced some gold coins to pay for the drinks. Some of his enemies had Swilling and his partner, George Munroe, arrested and charged with the robbery. The court ignored their defense that they had just returned to Gillett after selling one of Swilling's mining claims, and that the gold coins came from the sale. Swilling was sentenced to Yuma Penitentiary.

"I saw Jack Swilling in the penitentiary at Yuma," states another Arizona pioneer, William (Billy) Fourr, in his reminiscences, "but the guards would not let me talk to him. They said Jack would go crazy when he saw an old-timer. His whiskey and morphine were taken from him and that, with the injustice of the charge against him, killed him." And so Jack Swilling passed away in Yuma prison in 1878. A few months later the charges against him were conclusively proven to be false.

Duppa's given name was Bryan Philip Darrell, "Darrell" being his mother's maiden name. Arizonans called him "Lord" and "Count" because of stories that Duppa was a titled Englishman, harum-scarum son of British nobility paid to stay away from England, and a "remittance man" because of this payment. He was well-educated, familiar with the classics, and spoke several languages fluently. After Duppa's death, a Phoenix man made inquiries into his background, the findings finally setting the stories about him straight.

Discovered was the fact that Darrell Duppa was in the eleventh generation of landed British gentry, not nobility but of considerable holdings and wealth. The family name was originally "d'Uphaugh," but even they used the Duppa spelling. Born in Paris on October 9, 1832, Darrell received a classical education at Cambridge. He went to New Zealand to meet his uncle, George Duppa, where he acquired some mining stocks. Presumably, some of these stocks were in mines near Prescott, to where he traveled from New Zealand. In a rare moment of expansiveness, he once confided in a friend that the voyages were filled with

Drawing depicting the first building erected in Phoenix, Hancock's Store at the northwest corner of First and Washington Streets. It also housed city and county offices and was a general meeting place. (Courtesy Arizona State Archives)

adventurous side trips. He had wandered to Wickenburg where he joined with Swilling in the Salt River irrigation venture.

Many are the stories of Duppa's suggesting "Phoenix" as the name of the new community. In the files of McClintock, the historian, is this version:

In the fall of 1869 Swilling, Duppa, John Larsen of the original ditch company and one of the pioneer Starar brothers, Jake or Andrew, were sitting on the bank of a newly-constructed canal. They were writing a company communication, an order for supplies, to Prescott. When the letter was complete, a question arose.

"It goes to Prescott, but whence does it come?"

"We have no name for this place," one said, "so let's give it a name. Will someone suggest a name?"

"Let's call it 'Stonewall,' " said Swilling, a Southerner, with General "Stonewall" Jackson in mind. Starar sarcastically said, "Yes, call it 'Stonewall'." That displeased Swilling, who said, "Well, someone name it."

Starar then suggested "Salina," but Larsen objected that it suggested a salt marsh, and they should not give the impression that the valley was a salt swamp or alkali flat. Then Duppa spoke up.

"This canal was partly built in a time forgotten now," he said. "Pre-historic cities, now in ruins, are all around you. A pre-historic civilization existed in this valley. Let the new city arise from the ashes of these ruins, and let us call it 'Phoenix.' " After Duppa had explained the meaning of the name, all four agreed that was the very name, and so the address "Phoenix, Salt River Valley" was written for the first time.

If this event actually transpired, the time given for it is wrong, and it had to have occurred in the spring of 1868, because in May of that year an election precinct called "Phoenix" was formed in the settlement. And you can bet your bottom dollar the conversation wasn't all that formal; we're talking rugged frontiersmen here, and Duppa himself was no panty-waist. He had been on Indian fighting expeditions, and had the undying respect of his rough companions. Upon his arrival in Prescott, one had ridiculed the clothing Duppa was wearing and continued his insults until Duppa said, "I have nothing against you and don't want to hurt you, but to show you that I am not afraid I will fight you a duel." So it was arranged, each chose his second and stood at 50 paces with drawn revolvers. At a signal both fired until their revolvers were empty, but no shot took effect. Duppa then suggested they reload and keep firing until one fell, but by now his opponent was happy to call off any further dueling.

Duppa's "remittance" appears not to have been payment by his family to stay away from England, but rather from his share of the family's very considerable income from its lands and other properties. One source says that the amount was paid quarterly and administered by Duppa's lawyer, Capt. W. A. Hancock. Hancock, incidentally, was one of the most prominent of early settlers. He had first arrived in Arizona with the Union's California Column, then assigned to Fort McDowell after the Civil War. Discharged from the army, he was post sutler at McDowell for a time. He took out a homestead and was also a surveyor and businessman.

"Phoenix" as a name for the new community was first legally used when the Board of Supervisors of Yavapai County (Maricopa County was not formed until February, 1871) added it as an election precinct on May 4, 1868, naming it the Phoenix precinct. With people fast arriving now, filing on 160-acre homesteads, and some businesses being opened, the selection and laying out of a townsite became the topic of acrimonious debate. Some wanted it around Hellings Mill at about 32nd and Van Buren Streets, where

Rare photo of Washington Street, Phoenix, about 1875-76. Taken from southeast corner of Central Ave. and Washington, looking east on Washington. Low, flat-roofed building at the extreme left with people in front was Goldman's store. Beyond it the large, shingle-roofed building housed Johnny George's Capitol Saloon, a restaurant and barber shop, with the Capitol Hotel upstairs. Beyond the Capitol were Henry Morgan's Indian goods store and Hancock's store. Note flat-roofed dwellings at right on the south side of the street, and the town ditch in the foreground. The cottonwood trees were planted by pioneer Luke Monihon. Photo identification by Phoenix pioneer Neri Osborn. (Courtesy Arizona State Archives)

Dennis and Murphy had a saloon and Capt. Hancock a small store. Jack Swilling badly wanted it there, as his house was at the southwest corner of what is now 40th and Washington Streets. Many others wanted it located further to the west, so a mass meeting was called, held on October 20, 1870, at the house of John Moore.

As a result of the meeting, Darrell Duppa, Martin P. Griffin and John Moore were appointed as a committee to select a suitable spot of unoccupied public lands as the townsite. They chose the half-section known as the north one-half of section eight, township one north, range three east, bounded by today's Van Buren and Harrison Streets, Seventh Street and Seventh Avenue, because it was so covered with Indian ruins as to be considered useless for farming.

Even then, the reminiscences of Neri Osborn state that when the townsite was being looked over by his father, John P., and John T. Alsap, president of the townsite commissioners, they found two men quarreling over who would file homesteads on it. They bought the men out for $25 each and persuaded them to file elsewhere. This $50 was included in the entire cost of obtaining and filing on the townsite, which came to $550.

Alsap and the other two Salt River Valley Town Association commissioners, J. P. Perry and James Murphy, employed Capt. Hancock to survey and plat the newly-chosen Phoenix location. He began in November, 1870, the same month in which former Tucson businessman Charles T. Hayden moved to the south bank of the Salt River, ten miles to the east, to establish the settlement which evolved into the city of Tempe. While Hancock was surveying, the town commissioners were attempting to attract businesses by granting concessions within the townsite. One of these was at the spot where the Luhrs building later would rise. It was given to William and Nick Bichard of Adamsville near Florence to build a steam flour mill. Construction began late in December, 1870, and the first flour was ground in July, 1871. Three months later arsonists burned it to the ground with a loss of $10,000, and it was never rebuilt.

By December, Hancock had completed enough of his survey to permit the first sale of town lots to raise money to continue with the work of surveying. The Prescott *Miner* newspaper on December 7, 1870, carried an advertisement, "Great Sale of Town Lots at Phoenix, Arizona, on the 23rd and 24th of December, 1870. One-third of the purchase money will be required at the time of sale, the balance when the title is made." Another article in the *Miner* of January 7, 1871, reported that the lots had sold for from $20 to $142.50, with an average of $43.50. Judge Berry of Prescott bought the first lot, at the southwest corner of First and Washington Streets, for $103. The town had 500 to 600 people, three merchants, one brewer, and one hotel keeper, and a second lot sale was to be held January 21, 1871. That sale saw fewer lots going, though the usual price asked was $11 for corners and $7 for interior lots. Two lots were reserved for schools, two were given to churches, and one to the Masonic Order.

Maricopa County was created on February 12, 1871, and competition immediately arose for the location of the county seat. It might be supposed that it would fall naturally to Phoenix, but there was enough pressure from the original small settlement near 32nd and Van Buren Streets, called Mill City, to again force a vote. Neri Osborn hinted that skullduggery was afoot in this excerpt from his reminiscences: "Was trouble in 1871 when county had been formed and county seat was to be selected with name of Phoenix. Bill Hellings had the mill quarter, favored by upper

North side of Washington, Phoenix, circa 1875-76, looking east from Central Avenue. A. D. Lemon's home and law office, Heinson's Bakery, Salari's Restaurant. (Courtesy Historical Collection of Herb and Dorothy McLaughlin)

settlers. Jack Swilling had corralled a lot of Mexicans at a barbeque (to vote his way.) John Dennis got among the Mexicans and switched their tickets. When the vote was announced, Swilling shot the boss Mexican." Swilling was up to his old tricks again, illustrated by another story involving him and the able John T. Alsap, attorney, chairman of the town commissioners, probate judge who issued the first deeds to town lots, and

Phoenix's first mayor. Alsap was in a saloon when Swilling began "clearing out the place." Alsap calmly kept his seat and continued reading a newspaper. When Swilling asked, "Aren't you afraid of me?" Alsap was said to have replied, "No, Jack, if I was I would kill you," an answer that got him the immediate respect of Swilling.

While Hancock was continuing his survey, completed in the fall of 1871, buildings were already going up. Washington Street between Central and First Street was at the beginning the principal business center. At the northwest corner of First and Washington, on the west half of the lot, was the first building, of adobe. It was occupied by Hancock's general store, county offices, and was the town hall and general meeting house. Next west was an Indian goods store owned by Henry Morgan and Dan Dietrich of Morgan's Ferry on the Maricopa Wells road south of town. West of that was Johnny George's saloon in a building called "The Capitol," with a second story in which Charlie Salari ran the Capitol Hotel. Further west, with some vacant lots interspersed, were Goldman Brothers first mercantile store, Skirrow's saloon, Salari's restaurant, Hienson's bakery, and A. D. Lemon's law office.

Across the street, on the southwest corner of First and Washington Streets, was a large building on four lots which first housed Miguel Peralta's mercantile business, then an alley which later was called "Cactus Way." Next was a business building in which was George Loring's store called "Loring's Bazar," in which was the Wells-Fargo office. The Wells-Fargo agent was Madison "Matt" Larkin, succeeded in that position by Loring, who named his son Madison after his friend Larkin. Next west was the Palace Saloon, then from an old picture what appears to be a long lodging house with separate doors opening on Washington Street. All of these were adobe except the Peralta building, built later, which was brick.

Some of the first buildings and businesses were owned by men from Prescott, seat of Yavapai County, and in 1864 the first territorial capital. Among them were the Goldwaters, Michael, Morris and Julius, the above-mentioned Miguel Peralta, and Michael Wormser. The first telegraph office was in Michael Goldwater's store, with Michael the telegrapher, but the store was sold to Smith and Stearns whose flour mill occupied most of the southwest quarter of that block.

Capt. Hancock was appointed the first sheriff of the new Maricopa County until May, 1871, when an election was held to fill county offices. Gunfire broke out over the election of a new sheriff, and Arizona pioneer L. E. Williamson, an employee of one of the men in the shoot-out, told what happened. Williamson had come to Arizona from Texas, had worked for King Woolsey at Stanwick's Station on the old Gila trail, but in 1871 was working for Gus Chenoweth, the Democratic nominee for sheriff. The Republican nominee was Jim Favorite. While Chenoweth was on a trip to the old Maricopa Wells stage station on the Gila trail some sixteen miles south of Phoenix, Favorite circulated a story of a mutual agreement he had reached with Chenoweth. The arrangement was that whoever was elected sheriff, Favorite or Chenoweth, would appoint the other as his deputy.

"Chenoweth was superintendent of the Salt River Canal," recounted Williamson, "and I was working for him. When he got back from Maricopa Wells and heard the story Favorite was telling, he went out to Favorite's ranch to ask him about it. Favorite denied having told the story but he refused to make a public statement denying it. In the quarrel that followed, he shot at Chenoweth with a double-barreled shotgun but missed him. The shot got so close that the wadding from the gun fell into a pocket of my coat, which I had loaned Chenoweth, and burned a hole in the bottom of it.

"Favorite then ran into a corral and Chenoweth, with a revolver shooting through the cracks, killed him. Chenoweth then withdrew from the race . . ."

Tom Barnum entered the race without opposition and was elected sheriff. Shortly thereafter, a Chilean named Joaquin got drunk and rode up and down the street, "disturbing the peace with a double-barreled shotgun." Barnum happened along, and deputized a man named Joe Phy to bring him in. Phy, the same man who in 1888 fought the gun duel with Peter Gabriel in Florence, commandeered a horse hitched by the sidewalk and started after the Chilean. A few minutes later he returned and told the sheriff that the body lay by the roadside a half-mile out.

Phoenix's first lynching occurred on July 3, 1873. The immediate cause of the lynching was the stealing of a cow by Mariano Tisnado, who was, however, already under heavy suspicion on well-justified circumstantial evidence of having killed a respected citizen, H. G. Griffin, in the previous month. The cow was stolen from rancher B. F. Patterson, her picket rope cut, and she was driven toward the butcher shop of one Refugio Subiate. About three hundreds yards from the shop, her head and horns were found by Patterson, who had followed the trail. Subiate confessed that he had bought the cow from Tisnado before daylight. Arrested and brought before the justice of the peace, Tisnado was found guilty of the theft and lodged in the hoosegow. Tom Hayes, who was then the sheriff, slept all night in the jail, knowing that feeling against Tisnado was running high. But at about nine o'clock the next morning the vigilantes moved in suddenly and in force. They took the prisoner and strung him up in broad daylight from a high gatepost at the Washington Street entrance to Jack Starar's corral at First Avenue and Washington.

Before the jail was built, prisoners held for minor offenses were simply chained to big iron staples, driven into a huge log behind the county offices. The story is told of an imposing citizen named Algernon "Babe" Dove, a large farm worker of Bunyonesque proportions and strength, and a legendary saloon brawler when he was drunk, which was often. One night Babe was arrested for drunkenness and chained to the log. Around midnight he became so thirsty he could no longer stand it. Babe shouldered the huge log and carried it to the saloon across the street, through the door, and demanded a drink. The astonished bartender instantly set one up on the bar. Babe downed it, carried the log back to its place, lay down beside it and went to sleep.

A monograph by historian McClintock in his files describes the increasing lawlessness in frontier Phoenix and a day of reckoning in 1879. Phoenix then was the supply point for scores of prospectors and promoters of mines operating in the rich mountains to the north. The Southern Pacific railroad had stopped construction work at Casa Grande, and many of its "camp followers" had gravitated to Phoenix. Mexican refugees, many of them far from the highest social classes, had also descended upon Phoenix, which then had about 1,500 residents, about half being Mexican.

There was a semi-organized vigilante committee around Phoenix, composed mostly of farmers, who had been active in the past. They had hanged several horse thieves, had run down and

*Phoenix **Daily Herald** newspaper office, picture probably taken in the winter-spring of 1881-82. The building was on the east side of Center Street between Washington and Jefferson Streets, north of the alley.* (Courtesy Arizona Historical Society)

planted half a dozen desperados near the junction of the Salt and Verde rivers, and kept sort of uneasy peace, but for a time seemed to become dormant. Men were being wounded and killed until a "man for breakfast" no longer aroused interest. The semi-weekly *Herald* seldom gave more than a half-column to a murder. The Gilmer, Salisbury & Company's stage line, that furnished transportation to the railroad terminal at Maricopa, thirty miles south, was being held up about twice a week. Even its agent, Jim Stewart, and a famous messenger named Gilson were obliged to throw up their hands on several occasions; driver Billy Blankenship tried to hold off the road agents once and had his hands filled with buckshot for his pains.

Racial tensions between Americans and Mexicans also were high, and they were the trigger of the explosion. Sunday horse races on the main street were a favorite diversion. One summer Sunday about half of the population was stretched along Washington Street in two long lines, pressing toward the street center, looking westward to the start of two racing ponies. Down the course came a horseman galloping, apparently to clear the way, but actually running amok. In his hand was a long cavalry saber, with which he was savagely slashing right and left as he yelled "Muerto a los gringos!" ("Death to the Americans!")

He dashed down the street and escaped before the crowd had fully understood his murderous intentions. Several people had been wounded, two of them seriously. The horseman was identified as one Jesus Carillo, but known from then on as the "Saber Slasher." An intrepid lawman, Henry Garfias, trailed him far below the Mexican border into Sonora, brought him back without the formality of extradition, and lodged him in a Phoenix jail to await the results of the wounds he had inflicted.

A week early in August, 1879, turned out to be an especially lively one, even for frontier Phoenix. There were six murders, two of especial atrocity that enraged the citizenry. A prominent farmer a few miles west of the city, Luke Monihon, was driving home at dusk one evening when he was shot in the back from behind a roadside screen of brush. The team of farm horses trotted on home, and as they stopped at his door his wife came out and found the lifeless body of her husband in the wagon bed. It didn't take long to run down the murderer, named Keller, with whom Monihon had previously had trouble. Indian trailers followed his track to the house of one Willcoxen, where he had lodgings, and he was tossed into the pokey.

The reminiscences of A. N. Porter, once a bartender in Jack Walter's saloon, recounted the details of the other murder. A popular owner of another saloon, Johnny LaBar, was attempting to rouse a mob to lynch Keller, and came into Walters' saloon. He shouted, "All you blankety-blanks come up and take a drink!" Everyone did except one man with chin whiskers who was sitting reading a newspaper. When LaBar repeated his command, this man who was named McGloskey, said, "You didn't tell me." LaBar replied that he certainly had. "You said 'all you blankety-blanks,' " replied McGloskey, "and I don't drink with them." LaBar grabbed McGloskey by the chin whiskers, dragged him to the bar, and slammed his head against it. At this the enraged McGloskey drew a knife and stabbed LeBar to death. McGloskey wound up in the jail with Keller.

The next day the "Saber Slasher" attempted a jail break. One of the floor boards in his cell was loose; when the cell was swept, the

Goldman's general merchandise store in early Phoenix. Man with moustache and derby hat in left foreground is Adolf Goldman. (Courtesy Arizona Historical Society)

dirt was swept under it. Holding this board as a club, the "Slasher" was waiting when jailor Hy McDonald opened the cell to allow an attorney named Stephenson into it. The crosspiece above the cell door averted the "Slasher's" blow, and McDonald shot him twice, killing him. The news of this caused an immediate stir of discontent among the Mexican population, and messengers were hurriedly dispatched to all parts of the valley to assemble the vigilantes.

Bright and early the next morning the Mexicans began to assemble around the plaza. There seemed to be hundreds of their ponies tied to the huge cottonwood trees that shaded the block. The riders were armed with an assortment of old firearms, mainly dragoon pistols. The vigilantes, however, were gathering in overwhelming force on Jefferson Street. All were armed with rifles and revolvers, with an occasional bowie knife in the boot. A farmer named Marion Slankard was their captain. Down First Street and around into Washington swung the heavily-armed column of over a hundred determined men. All was quiet in their ranks and on the crowded sidewalks. They marched past the alley and up to the little adobe courthouse, filing in without resistance. The officers, knowing what was coming, had discreetly found occupations elsewhere. Hy McDonald demurred at the suggestion that he hand over the keys, but was convinced of the wisdom of it at the point of a dozen revolvers.

About ten prisoners were in the jail, but the vigilantes took only Keller and McCloskey. It was about ten o'clock in the morning, and they selected the fourth and fifth cottonwoods from First Street on Washington as hanging trees. The men were put separately into an express wagon, allowed a few parting words, and the wagon driven from under them. Keller fainted. He was dragged from the wagon by the rope, and slowly strangled. McCloskey, watching this, was put into the wagon last. When the wagon began to move, he stepped up on the tailgate and sprang into the air. The drop at the end of the rope snapped his neck and he died instantly. The crowd was very quiet, but one said, "Why, the son of a gun must of been hanged before. He knew just how to do it."

McCloskey was barely gone when two more figures were stood up in the box of the express wagon. They were two Mexican merchants who for several days had been preaching a "crusade" against the gringos. They had been captured from among their partisans by a flanking movement of the vigilantes. Slankard spoke good Spanish, and made himself quite plain. Pointing to the swinging bodies, he warned that their fate would be the same if they uttered another inflammatory word. They were then released, and the insurrection of the Mexicans was over. The vigilantes then turned their attention to cleaning out the town of its undesirable American element, too. Everyone suspected of being a tough or crook was given a canteen and a warning. None disobeyed. Their departure was swift, many of them finding new fields of operations in the mining camp just beginning called Tombstone.

This riotous day, according to McClintock, had its effect on the lawbreakers and outlaws. "For years thereafter," he wrote, "Phoenix was as quiet a town as one could find in the staid New England states. This gratifying result was directly due to the vigilantes. That they accomplished a work of good is incontestable. They presented the law with a peaceful city and neighborhood, and peaceful it remained."

Historian McClintock, a fine and highly respected man, was wrong about that. It didn't remain peaceful, but things were dull for a while, so we will just leave you with this thought-provoking

South side of Washington Street, Phoenix, looking west toward Central from corner of alley west of First Street. Store building and Wells-Fargo office, Palace Saloon (narrow white building), and row of adobe dwellings facing Washington. (Courtesy Arizona Historical Society)

tidbit about the legislative process in Arizona that endures to this day:

J. D. Rumberg of Maricopa County was a member of the territorial legislature in the session of 1879. He was occasionally inclined to be cranky, so the members of that not overly sedate body were not especially amazed when he introduced a bill to prohibit horse racing in the Territory of Arizona. On second reading, a member from Pima County offered an amendment exempting Pima County from the provisions of the bill. Other amendments followed fast until Maricopa County alone remained. Then up rose John T. Alsap, prominent Phoenix resident and member of the legislature, Rumberg's colleague. He solemnly moved to amend by striking from the bill all mention of Maricopa County save so much as lay in the northeast quarter of section 34, township one north, range two east. This passed without opposition, and from that date it became unlawful to race horses upon the quarter section owned by J. D. Rumberg northwest of Phoenix.

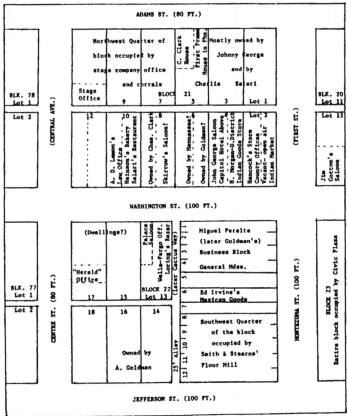

Phoenix Business District, c. 1875

Phoenix Business District, circa 1875-1876

BLOCK 20
Lot 12 — Jim Cotton's Saloon. Official records spell name "Cotten."

BLOCK 21
Lot 2, west half — Hancock's Store, the first building on the townsite, of adobe opened by William Smith, July 1871. Also served as county offices, town hall, and general meeting place. (History of Phoenix, by the city of Phoenix). Lot 2, east half —"The portion of the lot between (the) store and First Street was vacant except for a large number of cottonwood trees. The Maricopa Indians used this space as a public market for melons, ollas, and other merchandise which they brought to Phoenix for sale." (Reminiscenses of Charles M. Clark.)

Lot 4, east half — Owned by Henry Morgan and Dan Dietrich (county records) who had an Indian goods store there (reminiscences of Charles M. Clark.) Lot 4, west half — Owned by John George (county records) who "had a saloon and lodging house in what was called The Capitol, a two-story adobe." The lodging house was run by Charlie Salari. (Reminiscenses of Charles M. Clark.)

Lot 6 and east half of lot 8 — speculative and unconfirmed, based on various references to ownership of lots in this block in reminiscenses of Charles M. Clark and other pioneers. Clark also says that "in 1876 . . . Charlie Skirrow started a neat little saloon about where Ratner's Store now stands on the north side of Washington between Central and First Street."

Lot 8, west half — Owned by Charles M. Clark (county records.) Probably vacant, as his reminiscenses do not mention his building anything there, and he did run his store in the Hancock building. Clark mentions that there were several vacant lots in the block. Lot 10 — An old picture shows A. D. Lemon's law office and Heinson's Bakery on this spot, and there is mention of Salari's Restaurant in the Heinson bakery building. Lot 12 — No indication of what was there in 1875-76.

Lots 1, 3, 5 — No indication of buildings, but county records show several sales of lots and portions of them from John George to Charlie Salari.

Lot 5 — speculation that this is the location of the Charles M. Clark house from his reminiscenses, which state, "The first frame, or lumber, house to be erected in the Salt River Valley was built for the writer (Clark) by George H. Rothrock on an Adams Street lot directly opposite the entrance of the Adams Hotel."

Lots 7, 9, 11 — "Along about 1876-77 . . . the overland stage company built their office building and corral on the northwest quarter of the block, from the alley on the east side of Centre Street to the corner of Adams Street . . . The office building . . . was located on the corner of the alley between Washington and Adams."

BLOCK 22

All lots on streets opposite and facing the Court House Square and town Plaza were 25 feet wide; all other lots were 50' wide. According to the "History of Phoenix," distributed by the city, "in 1874 downtown lots were selling for $7 to $11 each." The difference was $11 for corners and $7 for interior lots. The first sales of lots, at auction, brought more. The first lot sale, an auction on December 7, 1870, "resulted in a sale of sixty-one lots at an average price of $48 each. The first lot was purchased by Judge William Berry of Prescott. It was the southwest corner of First Street and Washington, and he paid the rather steep price of $116."

Lots 1, 2, 3, 4 — Though the reminiscences of some pioneers refer to a business block built by Miguel Peralta but later taken over by Goldman Brothers as being at the northwest corner of Central and Washington, the records of the county recorder show this property as being Lots 1 through 4 of Block 22. This would place the building at the southwest corner of First Street and Washington. A sketch of Phoenix in 1895 by C. J. Dyer shows this building (then called the Irvine Building) at First Street and Washington.

Lot 6 (may have been 5 or 7, could not be found in county records) — "The tienda-barata (Mexican goods store) of E. Irvine was in the middle of the block on the west side of first street between Jefferson and Washington." (Reminiscenses of Charles M. Clark.)

Lots 8 through 12 — "Smith and Stearns were running a store and flour mill on the northwest corner of First and Jefferson." (Reminiscenses of Charles M. Clark.) The Dyer sketch shows it taking in the entire quarter of the block.

Lot 13, east 2/3 — Entire lot owned by George Loring (county records.) An old picture shows the east portion occupied by "Loring's Bazar." A sign painted on the side says "Wells-Fargo" office.

Lot 13, west 1/3 — The picture shows it occupied by the Palace Saloon.

Lots 15 & 17 — No indication of what was there, except that the above picture seemed to show a long lodging building with doors, facing Washington Street. This is merely speculation. The Dyer sketch identifies a building on Central avenue, with a lot between it and the alley, as the office of the "Phoenix Herald" newspaper. The reminiscences of historian James H. McClintock indicate that in later years, after the stage company had moved away, the newspaper took over the former stage company office building between Washington and Adams Streets, north of the alley.

Lots 14, 15, and 16, Block 22, were owned by Adolph Goldman (county records.)

On the south side of Jefferson Street, not shown in the sketch, were the Luhrs Wagon Shop and George Rothrock's photographic studio at the southeast corner of Montezuma (First Street) and Jefferson (county records).

Bibliography
and Suggested Reading List

Ahnert, Gerald. *Retracing the Butterfield Overland Trail Through Arizona.* Los Angeles: Westernlore Press, 1973.

Barnes, Will C. *Arizona Place Names.* Ed. Bryd Granger. Tucson: University of Arizona Press, 1960.

Breakenridge, William. *Helldorado.* Boston: Houghton-Mifflin, 1928.

Browne, J. Ross. *Adventures in the Apache Country.* New York: Harper and Bros., 1869.

Buchanan, James E. *Phoenix: A Chronological and Documentary History, 1875-1976.* Dobbs Ferry, (N.Y.): Oceana Publications, Inc., 1978.

Esenwein, William. *The Private Empire of Charlie P. Stanton.* Stanton (Ariz.): Privately published, 1972.

Falk, Odie B. *Arizona: A Short History.* Norman: University of Oklahoma Press, 1970.

Farish, Thomas. *History of Arizona.* Phoenix: Flimer Bros., 1915.

Hawkins, Helen B. *A History of Wickenburg to 1875.* Wickenburg (Ariz.): Maricopa County Historical Society, 1971.

Lauer, Charles D. *Old West Adventures in Arizona.* Phoenix: Golden West Publishers, 1989.

McLaughlin, Herb & Dorothy. *Phoenix 1870-1970.* Phoenix: Arizona Photographic Associates, 1970.

Murbarger, Nell. *Ghosts of the Adobe Walls.* Los Angeles: Westernlore Press, 1964.

Parker, Stanley W. *Southwestern Arizona Ghost Towns.* Las Vegas: Nevada Publications, 1981.

Peplow, E. H. *Taming of the Salt.* Phoenix: Salt River Project, 1979.

Sobin, Harris. *Florence Townsite, A. T.* Tucson: Isbell Printing Co., 1977.

Stratton, E. O. *Pioneering in Arizona: The Reminiscences of Emerson Oliver Stratton.* Ed. John A. Carroll. Tucson: Arizona Historical Society, 1964.

Summerhayes, Martha. *Vanished Arizona.* Salem (Mass.): Salem Press, 1911.

Trimble, Marshall. *Arizona Adventure.* Phoenix: Golden West Publishers, 1982.

Trimble, Marshall. *In Old Arizona.* Phoenix: Golden West Publishers, 1985.

Index of People and Places

Other Books by Charles D. Lauer

ARIZONA TRAILS & TALES
True Adventures in Arizona's Old West

Stories of true events and forgotten places in Arizona. Visit scenes of the past, see them as they are today and relive the historic adventures.
5 1/2 X 8 1/2 - 192 Pages...$14.95

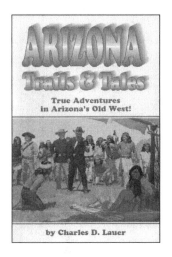

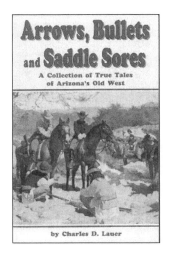

ARROWS, BULLETS and SADDLE SORES
True Tales of Arizona's Old West

Fascinating and true stories about events, places and people from Arizona's history. Read about the Wickenburg Massacre, The Earps' Wives and Women, Gun Battle at Stockton Ranch, Battle of Apache Pass and more! Includes maps and photos.
5 1/2 X 8 1/2 - 184 Pages...$9.95

OLD WEST ADVENTURES IN ARIZONA

In the Arizona Territory men played for keeps! It was a place where the romance of stagecoach travel was interrupted by murder from ambush...where raiding was a way of life. The place names of Arizona's history still ring with vibrant memories of a glorious past.
5 1/2 X 8 1/2 - 176 Pages...$9.95

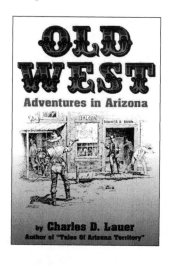

QTY	TITLE	PRICE	TOTAL
	Arizona Cook Book	9.95	
	Arizona Adventure	9.95	
	Arizona Legends and Lore	9.95	
	Arizona Territory Cook Book	6.95	
	Arizona Trails and Tales	14.95	
	Arizona Trivia	8.95	
	Arizoniana	9.95	
	Arrows, Bullets and Saddle Sores	9.95	
	Billy The Kid Cook Book	7.95	
	Cowboy Cook Book	9.95	
	Cowboy Slang	9.95	
	Ghost Towns in Arizona	12.95	
	Grand Canyon Cook Book	9.95	
	Haunted Arizona: Ghosts of the Grand Canyon State	12.95	
	Haunted Highway: The Spirits of Route 66	12.95	
	Jackalope Tales	6.95	
	Old West Adventures in Arizona	9.95	
	Sleeping With Ghosts: AZ Ghost Hunters Guide	12.95	

US Shipping & Handling Add	1-3 Books: 5.00
[for non-domestic ship rates, please call]	4-9 Books: 7.00
	9+ Books: 7.00 + 0.25 per book
	AZ residents add 8.3% sales tax

Please make checks payable to: (US funds only) Total: _____
Golden West Publishers
4113 N. Longview,
Phoenix, AZ 85014

☐ Check or money order enclosed
☐ MC ☐ VISA ☐ Discover ☐ American Express Verification Code:_____

Card Number:_____ Exp._____
Signature: _____
Name_____Phone: _____
Address _____
City_____State_____ZIP _____
Email _____ Prices are subject to change.

Visit our website or call us toll free for a free catalog of all our titles!